Child
of
Light

A TRUE STORY

✳

By
LORI GERSHON

AuthorHouse™
1663 Liberty Drive, Suite 200
Bloomington, IN 47403
www.authorhouse.com
Phone: 1-800-839-8640

AuthorHouse™ UK Ltd.
500 Avebury Boulevard
Central Milton Keynes, MK9 2BE
www.authorhouse.co.uk
Phone: 08001974150

First published by AuthorHouse 08/01/2006

ISBN :1-4259-5607-6 (sc)

Printed in the United States of America
Bloomington, Indiana

This book is printed on acid-free paper.

Cover and interior design by the Legwork Team.

Bloomington, IN  Milton Keynes, UK

authorHOUSE®

✳

*To Edie, my mentor and spiritual mother, I love you.
May our story raise the consciousness in the world and
honor who you represented in your life. I know that you
are continuing your work on the other side.*

✳

Acknowledgements

✳

To the Source of all there is, thank you for your spiritual blessings. Thank you for the abundant energy that was needed to write this story in those solitary hours. Thank you, Jerry, for our children Jeff and Aaron. I appreciate your generosity for managing without me at times. Josef, your support and encouragement means the world to me. Ann, your faith in my story was unwavering. Thank you, Legwork Team, for picking up all the loose ends and for meeting my deadlines.

Foreword

✳

About halfway into the writing of this story, while brushing his teeth before bed, my almost-five-year-old son said, "Mommy, when I was a baby, I knew everything. Now I don't know everything."

"Really," I said. "That's interesting. What did you know then?"

He responded, "That God lives." I smiled internally, a radiant smile, a smile which affirmed a truth I hold dear.

I believe all babies come into the world conscious of their connection to the One Mind, Universal Intelligence, the Great I Am, or God. Through our children, we can learn many important life lessons so that we, too, become and then live our lives more consciously aware of our connection to our source. *Child of Light* is the true story of my family's journey, a two-year ordeal forever embedding in our minds an impressive universal truth.

Chapter One

*

July 4, 1990. The annual Fourth of July celebration with my husband Jerry's family was well underway. I was first exposed to this landmark event five years ago, one month before Jerry and I got married, and believe me, I felt like I was in a crash course for a foreign immersion program of some sort. Oh, everyone spoke English and was quite friendly; there were just so many of them. The six children Jerry's grandmother and grandfather had raised over the years had multiplied into thirty-five first cousins, counting spouses, and at least another twenty-one second cousins. Magnifying my culture shock was the fact that I am an only child coming from parents who had but one sibling each.

This Fourth of July brought some new challenges; I was less than a week away from my due date, for which I received a fair amount of caution from many of my husband's aunts and uncles. Jerry's conventional family held that a woman should not travel outside her immediate vicinity at this late stage of pregnancy. But this was my second child and I was a contemporary woman with a non-conventional flair. I often stepped many strides outside the parameters of their conventionality, and sometimes way to the left to top it off. To be pregnant and tuned into a woman's body, with all of its rhythms and cycles, is to know whether to risk traveling nearly a hundred miles for a Fourth of July bash.

Some half hour after our arrival and the hugs and kisses from many of the aunts, uncles, and cousins, that old familiar sensation of hunger for two sneaked up on me, so I left Jerry and our son, Jeffrey, and walked towards the buffet table only to cross paths with a family member to whom I had not yet said hello, cousin Mark. "It looks like you're about to drop that baby any day now," he critiqued. "Are you doing it at home again, like you did with Jeffrey?"

"Absolutely. I wouldn't do it any other way," I replied unabashedly. Mark, a young and quite successful anesthesiologist working at a major New York City hospital, had a most unsettling knack of luring me into heated conversations about my non-conventional, holistic ideals. Five years of experience with him had taught me to take these conversations with a grain of salt and then go my merry way.

"Did you have any sonograms done?" he asked. "You are concerned about birth defects and congenital abnormalities, aren't you?" It was more a pedantic statement of his position on the subject than a straightforward, well-meaning question.

"I'm not in any of your high-risk groups," I responded. "I'm still way under forty. Besides, I have

perfect faith that what's meant to be is meant to be."
I had come to be a real believer in this philosophy over
the past ten years.

I hold strong to a belief that our birth experiences
profoundly affect our lives by laying down the
foundation upon which our personalities are formed.
Jerry and I had thoroughly researched this area and
had decided to birth at home to provide our children a
loving, gentle, and respectful entrance into the physical
world. Some researchers say that our birth experience
forms our opinions of the world. A gentle start will
enable a child to begin life with a positive expectation
of the world, in contrast to the child born through
conventional approaches employing sonograms,
labor-inducing drugs, C-sections, and forceps. These
subtleties of the personality affect how we create our
lives and how our relationships are patterned. The
French obstetrician, Dr. Frederick LeBoyer, author
of the pioneering book "Birth Without Violence,"
placed his newborn babies in a very warm tub of
water to simulate the intrauterine environment. This
softened the transition from the intimate and aqueous
environment of the mother's womb to the physical
separation, atmospheric breathing, and substantially
lower temperature of the atmospheric environment.

I had obviously silenced Mark by my comment.
I had kept myself out of the medical community's
high-risk groups by adhering to a well-rounded vegan
diet, exercising daily, and subscribing to the tenets of
positive thinking.

"And, I take really good care of my body." Fuel for

my fire, I thought, as I served myself two bowlfuls of a lavish medley of fresh melons and berries. I popped one luscious raspberry into my mouth and threw a scornful glance down at his fat-laden cold cuts on a no-nutrition, white-flour roll.

As I turned towards three-year-old Jeffrey, being entertained by his father, Mark chidingly got the last word in. "I hope you have a back-up hospital, at least."

In these instances, being diplomatic with family can be a most difficult, if not impossible, feat. To choose a different path in life is to guarantee participation in at least one of these award-winning debates at family functions.

"My cousin gave you one of his famous dissertations," Jerry laughed. "Sounded to me like you maintained your ground most respectably."

Jerry and I hold common beliefs in many areas, particularly regarding holistic health and spiritual matters, and we had had more than our share of award-winning debates over our vegetarianism, spiritual beliefs, and alternative life practices. I just happened to be the one to defend our perspective this time.

Chapter Two

✳

Three nights after the party, our anticipation peaking, Jerry and I fell asleep in each other's arms to a bright moonlit night serenaded by summer's crickets. But a few hours later, I was abruptly roused from an already restless sleep by a sharp pain spreading across my lower abdomen. "Oh my God, Jerry, I'm getting my first contraction!" I jolted straight up and turned on the light.

Jerry, covering his head with the pillow, peered out from under a corner. "Should we call Roberta?" he asked.

Several breaths later, after doing rapid recall on my labor with Jeffrey and concluding that I was more confident this time around, I noticed the contraction had passed. "No, it's too early. I'm going back to sleep. I'd rather sleep through this part of labor so I'm rested for the real work." Labor was long with Jeffrey — forty two hours long — with seventeen of them in hard labor. Yet, we managed to birth him at home without a single intervention. I prayed it would take less time with this baby. At the same time, I knew I needed my sleep just in case history repeated itself, again requiring the tremendous concentration and long hours of some of the hardest work I'd ever done.

"Let me know if you need me, Sweets," Jerry mumbled, falling back to sleep rather immediately. I tossed and turned for at least an hour, jolting upright every ten minutes or so as my abdomen began to tighten. As I relaxed enough between contractions to get lulled into sleep, I had the funny thought that if there were an art to sleeping through labor contractions, I would be adept by night's end.

The last time I noticed the clock, it was five-thirty in the morning. I had finally drifted off to sleep just as the sun peered over the horizon, the birds chirping on a tree right outside my bedroom window.

"Good morning Mommy. Good morning Daddy." Jeffrey's joyful voice stepped right into my fitful dream. Every morning, at about seven o'clock, he burst into our room and jumped into bed with us. Remembering the previous night's activity, I immediately felt my belly, but felt no more contractions.

"Are you okay, Sweets?" Jerry asked.

"Well," I said, "I don't feel the contractions right now. I feel okay, though. I'll call Roberta just to play safe."

Roberta had been our midwife for Jeffrey's birth too; and while dialing her number, I chuckled to myself remembering how I cursed at her somewhere around the fortieth hour when she was probing with her hand to see how dilated I was.

"I woke you, didn't I?" I apologized.

"I had to get up anyway. What's up?" Roberta asked.

"I was having light labor contractions last night. Somehow I slept through most of it. Now, I'm not having any." I was half expecting to hear something that wasn't too encouraging.

"That's not uncommon, Lori. Go for a swim or something today. Even a long walk would be fine. No running, though. You can call my beeper if you go into labor."

I did as she said. I went for a five-mile walk in the morning and swam a mile later in the day. Friends often said my baby would be born with Nikes on. I had added nine months onto my already thirteen-year running and seven-year triathlon career, running and swimming throughout my entire pregnancy. I ran slower and walked up hills, but I got out there nonetheless. Roberta guided me on safety precautions.

Yet, with all that exercise, there were no more contractions that day.

I'm convinced someone up there has a very odd sense of humor. Even after all that exercise, I was awakened at about three in the morning again. I ignored the callings of Mother Nature, just as I had done the previous night, for I was not willing to be ill-prepared for the forthcoming hours of labor.

The following morning, perplexed, I was once again out of labor, trying to lift my spirits by joking with Jerry at how I had successfully conquered the sleep-depriving effects of labor. My frustration level was up a few notches from the day before, so I introduced a two-mile swim to that non-productive day.

As I settled into seductive sleep that night, my mind pondered the off-and-on nature of my labor. I prayed for a full night's sleep and a birth the next day. However, this night turned out to be a repeat performance of the last two, with contractions nearly every ten minutes between the hours of two and five. I barely budged when the contractions aroused me from my sleep. Had they been the real thing, I wouldn't have been able to sleep through them anyway.

But by dawn the following day, yes, day number three of this questionable birthing process, I was again not in labor. By now, I was totally frustrated and annoyed with myself. One night's interrupted sleep is one thing, but three nights is a whole other story. I was becoming testy. I now think this child was negotiating with God about coming through. I pondered a heated spiritual debate between the two of them:

"Why are you putting your mother through all this? You know she needs her sleep."

"With all due respect, God, I'd rather stay up here with you. I got used to the abundant light and love around here."

"But it's your time to go back, my son. It's important you continue your soul's evolution.

"But my parents-to-be, God, they're nuts. They don't eat meat. And she's planning to give birth to me at home! Can you believe it — in this day and age, with all the high-tech advances medicine has made?"

At this point, God would smile and say, "Everything's in divine order, not to worry, my son."

Divine order or not, it was time to take things

into my own hands a bit. A nicely paced run in July's humidity should jump-start my labor.

Five miles of mostly walking, some frustrated crying, and a few attempts to jog my body into labor left me feeling more disheartened and, if that weren't enough, powerless to affect any change. Just my karma, I thought, reflecting on an Eastern philosophical perspective presented to me many times, a philosophy which purports that our children are our gurus, or teachers, who have come to us to teach us important life lessons. I was definitely being taught two poignant lessons about trust and surrender before the little tike even came into the world. My pushing wasn't getting me what I wanted; my attempts at jogging granting me not even the slightest bit of tightening in my abdomen.

Chapter Three

✳

Then it happened. I started to get contractions around four in the afternoon and within one hour, right after Jerry came home, hard labor announced itself with brute force. By six, Roberta had come over, as had our baby-sitter, Marie, whose plan it was to take Jeffrey to her home for the time I would be in hard labor. Under Roberta's guidance, we had prepared Jeffrey with videos showing other three-year-olds and their siblings' births. Jeffrey had honest intentions of helping, but his idea of helping was climbing on my back while I groaned on the floor, kneeling on all fours. By this time, I was in real active labor, in celebration of and ecstatic for a painful journey which would end with a miracle.

My contractions persisted, and somehow I hung in as they mounted in intensity and came more frequently, to the point where my body had a scant thirty seconds to recoup between the onslaughts of pain. Although not to the extent I felt matched with the incredibly strenuous work I had been doing, the contractions were fruitful; by nine in the evening, Roberta announced I was dilated about five centimeters.

I sat up after Roberta examined me, waiting for the next contraction. Thirty seconds... a minute... ninety seconds... two full minutes. Roberta and I looked at one another, curiously. Three minutes, five minutes, seven and ten minutes passed. My labor had come to a dead halt, with no warning, and no apparent reason. It felt like my heart stopped, my mind gripped with an unsettling fear.

Jerry sat next to me as Roberta tended to the vital signs. My blood pressure, my heart rate, and the baby's heart rate were all steady, nothing explaining the immediate halt in my labor. I could sense Roberta's growing concern in her attempts to keep a measure of calm attached to the moment.

Hundreds of thoughts raced through my mind, my concern so consuming I couldn't think straight. Being this much out of control was paralyzing for me. I felt an urgency to move into my own space, to center myself, maybe just to move away from worried conversation; so I decided to change sitting surfaces, and went into the chamber where I do some of my best thinking, the bathroom. I must have sat there at least ten minutes, trying to gain some clarity about what was happening and why. I have a strong tendency to be totally mental at times, not taking things at face value, but rather processing information much like a computer does when fed a new disk. My mind searched for something, anything that could make sense out of three days of off-and-on labor, and now this — sudden hard labor working over a body and soul intent on delivering a baby, then reversing its intention and stopping.

In frustration, I cried out to God, "Why? Why are you allowing this to happen to me?" I felt powerless, painfully vulnerable, abandoned by a lifetime best friend. The trusting innocence in me fearfully withdrew and in the flash of a second, out came the angry justifier with the sole intention of shielding me from the pain of this injustice. "What do you want, God? Why are you doing this to me? I didn't do anything to deserve this."

Even though Roberta said the baby's vital signs were okay, maybe it was the baby. Maybe it didn't want to come from a spiritual into human form. Maybe that was why I was in and out of labor for three days.

My mind rehashed the past few days' events, straining for some shred of information that would help me understand why this was happening. Was I responsible in any way?

Devastated, I had nothing else to grab, my inner victim needed to blame, to hold responsible, someone or something. In a flash, all three possibilities occurred to me. Individually or collectively, God, Aaron, and/or I created this.

"Lori," Jerry called to me. I had lost track of time while in the battlegrounds of my mind. I got myself together and went out to sit next to him on the edge of the bed, my eyes red from the crying I had done in the bathroom. With great concern, Jerry put his arm around me, and tears spontaneously poured forth from my eyes, speaking the fear and utter confusion my words could not express.

"I don't think this baby wants to come through, Jerry. I don't know why, but it just feels like that."

Gently, with the soft care only my totally loving husband could provide, Jerry calmed me — me, the nervous wreck. Both my births brought out the best in Jerry. In general, I played the role of being the strong one in our relationship, by virtue of what was my somewhat dysfunctional need to be in control. I didn't have the strength or mental fortitude to keep up that act while I was in labor, and the very softening of my energies created the space for Jerry to be the strong one. Not that Jerry wasn't a bit nervous himself; he was fighting the same battle I was.

Within twenty minutes, labor started again, with quite a bang, just where it had left off. Within minutes, I was well entrenched in the productive contractions of hard labor, as if God said, "No more debating this, baby. It's time."

For the next thirty minutes, lying on my back propped up by numerous pillows and soothed with Jerry's loving shoulder and neck massages along with cool washcloths to wipe away the volumes of sweat, somehow I endured contractions more painful than I'd ever imagined. The excruciating pain strengthened my resolve, though, ending in confirmation from Roberta that I was fully dilated.

Magically, the baby-sitter showed up with my son. Jeffrey, two years and nine months old, asked animatedly, "Am I going to be a big brother, soon?" Good comic relief and well-timed, at that.

The contractions at this point were continual and

I began pushing, hoping to find enough strength to bring closure to this event. I motioned Jerry to usher Marie and Jeffrey out of the room for a few minutes, for I didn't want to concern Jeffrey as I writhed in pain, assuming crunched-up positions that helped me bear down. And the sounds that came forth from my belly and out my mouth enhancing the efficacy with which I pushed, I thought would certainly frighten him. Jerry went out with them, cajoling Jeffrey to get into pajamas; by the time he'd be done, the baby would be ready to be born.

At the precise moment I needed him, Jerry returned to the room, just as my strength was beginning to ebb. Roberta put a mirror between my legs so I could see my baby's head crowning. What an incredible perspective, the spreading apart of my most accommodating pelvis whose ligaments had started to relax three full months earlier in preparation for these majestic moments, just prior to my baby's descent down my birth canal.

I rested during the five-second reprieve I got between the fast-paced contractions and then continued pushing once again. Any control I had left was gone by this point, the contractions taking total control of my body. They came over me like waves in the ocean, crashing, one after the other, doing to my body precisely what needed to be done. A woman learns everything she needs to know about surrender in this stage of labor. It was time to just let go, let God, and let my body do what it innately knew to do.

More pushing, more breathing. I felt myself opening more and more, yearning to hold my baby. My bottom burned as it stretched to accommodate the baby's head pushing through.

Still more pushing, more opening. How much more, I thought, would I need to open? I reached down and felt my baby's head. Hair, I felt hair. The surface area I felt was like half the size of a tennis ball. Definitely not too much, but at least something. What a relief. For a second, I flashed on how much more I had to open so the whole head could come through. Gees, the burning was already pretty intense.

More pushing. I felt again, more of my baby's head. I was really starting to open wide. It felt like the whole top of the baby's head was just about through. I pushed until I could push no more, or so I thought, for I continued to find more strength from within to push one more time, each and every time. It was as if I was in a trance of some sort, just letting my body take over and lead me in its most magnificent dance.

The muscular tension I had to generate in my entire body to push had me sweating bullets and feeling like my eyes were bulging out of my head. I remembered how swollen my face had been from pushing Jeffrey out. Through the haze, I heard Roberta say, "Lori, slow the pushing a bit. Don't push your baby out yet. Jerry, are you ready to bring your baby into the world?" Jerry, a little scared and very excited, moved down to the foot of the bed.

Jeffrey and Marie came back into the room and sat near Jerry. Jeffrey was perched on Marie's lap waiting with all of us for the new baby to announce itself.

"Sit by me," Roberta said to Jerry, patting the

mattress just to her side. "Place your hands under your baby's head as it starts to come out. Lori, you're doing great. Easy go, don't push any more." Don't push? Absolutely impossible.

Roberta poured olive oil into her hands and massaged me, gently stretching me wider to accommodate my baby's head without tearing. I was grateful for the olive oil as this made unnecessary what most doctors do — episiotomies. "Don't push, Lori. I want to make sure the umbilical cord is free." I felt Roberta slip her hand in me. I didn't think I could open a centimeter more. "The umbilical cord is free. Easy go, though. I don't want you to tear. Don't push. Hold back the pushing of the contractions so your baby can come out slowly."

The pressure of my baby's head pushing its way out of my body, stretching me beyond any of my preconceived notions, burned fiercely. All I wanted to do was push my baby out and end the pain. "Easy, Lori. There you go. The head is just about through. Jerry, get ready to catch the shoulders."

All I could remember doing was squeezing down in a way that would slow my baby's exit out of my birth canal. Once my baby's shoulders were through, I let go. I couldn't hold on a second more. I felt my baby slide right out.

"It's a boy," Roberta announced, "You have another boy, Lori."

Eyes sparkling with immense pride and gratitude, Jerry held him up for me to see.

"Welcome to our family, little one," he said. "We've been waiting for you. We love you."

Jerry placed him on my chest while an amazed Jeffrey crawled up to the head of the bed and put his arm around me.

"What are you naming him?" Roberta asked.

"Aaron. After my grandmother and Jerry's brother."

Roberta took Aaron from me. "You ready to do the honors, Jerry?" She was referring to the cutting of the umbilical cord.

"Sure, I did it for Jeffrey, I could do it for Aaron."

And so Jerry clipped and cut the umbilical cord, creating the best of belly buttons, like only the best of dads could. Roberta cleaned Aaron, placed a baby blanket around his body and a cute little blue stocking hat on his head, then put him back in my yearning arms.

And that's how Aaron came into our world, some time shortly after eleven that evening. A thriving, seven-and-a-half pound boy, he was. The whole family was in bed; me, propped on pillows with Aaron trying to nurse; Jeffrey, his arm wrapped around my neck stroking Aaron's head with his other hand; and Jerry, sitting next to Jeffrey embracing all of us with a proud and loving look in his eyes.

"Am I a big brother now?" Jeffrey asked. Jerry and I gazed at each other, in awe of the moment, the miracle, and our love that made this possible.

Chapter Four

✳

With Jeffrey off at nursery school, Aaron and I set to the task of learning to nurse. Unlike his brother at this age, Aaron was very quiet and totally undemanding, a mother's dream, sleeping through the night from the onset. I thought it a gift.

I brought Aaron to our pediatrician, Dr. Kenefick, for his well baby check-up only to find out what I already knew: Aaron had two arms, two legs, healthy eyes and ears, strong reflexes, and his vital parts were intact. I described Aaron's feeding as a little slow, and then endured the sundry, unsolicited suggestions on breastfeeding from the nurse. I knew my territory. After all, Jeffrey nursed until he was two years and five months old, right through my fourth month of pregnancy with Aaron. I had the reputation for being a maven of sorts in the areas of breastfeeding and natural childbirth, particularly because of my exercising, vegetarianism, and nursing, while pregnant, a highly attached and very active two-year-old boy. My perception was that Aaron was different than Jeffrey, but should I have suspected something this early?

Aaron's feeding skills did not improve over the next few days. For some reason, he couldn't stay on my breast long enough to get adequate nutrition. Most newborns wake several times in the middle of the night due to unrelenting hunger; I had to wake mine for his feedings, feedings which lasted barely a minute, and then he would fall back asleep despite my attempts to keep him aroused.

Concerned and not feeling equipped to handle the challenges presented to me, I went back to the pediatrician, this time more willing to be taught some creative techniques by the nurse to help me get nourishment into Aaron. He was ten-days-old.

Back home again to practice.

But Aaron still didn't respond as well as he should have and I had to offer him my breast almost continually to keep him nourished. He just didn't have the staying power to suck for more than a minute or so. Very uneasy with how he was doing and feeling that the pediatrician had nothing else to offer in this area, I made an appointment with our homeopath, Dr. McCoy.

At this point, Aaron had just started to become very restless, as if he was uncomfortable in his body, even when he was sleeping. And he was napping far too often.

I got a late morning appointment with our homeopath. A graying older man, probably just past sixty, Dr. McCoy had an inordinately mild presence about him and a countenance that was almost devoid of any emotion. He worked quietly and I sensed a strong intuitive energy coming forth as he checked Aaron's heart and abdomen with his stethoscope. A homeopath focuses on treating the cause of a patient's condition, rather than the symptom, using natural substances and remedies to pulse the body into rebalancing itself. Our homeopath had the apparent additional qualification of being a board certified M.D.

After ten minutes examining a now cranky Aaron, Dr. McCoy walked into an adjoining room and returned with a tiny cylindrical glass bottle filled with tiny white spherical pellets. "Here, take these remedies for him," he said, "two pellets, every two hours. Try and drop it under his tongue if you can."

"But what's the problem?" I asked.

"I think colic. The remedies will help. Call me in a couple of days." He walked us to the door, obviously feeling he had made a complete diagnosis, but I was feeling extremely unsettled with my cranky child in my arms.

After we got home, feeling jittery myself, I put Aaron in a Snugli and went for a walk. He writhed as I walked along the country roads, his breathing sounding erratic, shallow, and rapid at the same time. Even though the homeopath seemed sure it was colic, the sensation in my gut told me he wasn't right.

I tried to keep myself calm and trust Dr. McCoy, whom I had relied upon faithfully for the past four years. I walked in the shade to avoid the hot August sun, praying Aaron would be okay. I couldn't keep myself calm any longer so three-quarters of a mile out on my walk, I turned around to go home. I was panicking.

It was an agonizing three-quarters of a mile back. Aaron was restless, every hasty step of mine apparently causing him more and more discomfort, and yet, no matter how I tried to hold him or even my gait, nothing made him comfortable. I questioned my choice to go to Dr. McCoy and questioned his diagnosis. With no way of really knowing, somehow I knew that colic didn't look like this. Babies with colic don't look so vulnerable and certainly don't whimper in pain and discomfort. I had colic as a baby and when my mother and father couldn't get me to stop crying, they'd put me in my crib and go out to the street for some peace and quiet. But they could still hear me. From that, I surmised that babies with colic scream, and scream loud. No, this was definitely not colic. I began to suspect it was something else, something serious.

At home, I found a friend of ours, a chiropractor in his professional life, sitting in our family room. Scott had been hiking in a state park nearby and came over to visit. I was feeling quite insecure being alone with Aaron in his current condition, so I appreciated his visit.

"Boy, his breathing doesn't sound good at all," he said.

"I'm scared, Scott," I said. "This has been going on for a few days already. He just doesn't seem to be thriving."

Scott and his wife, Susan, stand in about the same place as Jerry and I regarding conventional medicine. They used a midwife to birth their son too, and we both used Dr. McCoy as our homeopathic physician.

Scott looked at me with eyes that understood my fear.

"Do you think I ought to take Aaron to the pediatrician? Dr. McCoy thinks it's only colic. I don't think so, though. He looks too distressed."

He put a questioning, "I don't know" kind of look on his face. Then, obviously rethinking, it changed to concern. "I'd go to the pediatrician if I were you."

I called Dr. Kenefick's office. His nurse said to come over right away. "I'll tell Dr. Kenefick to expect you."

I called Jerry at work, my voice shaking as I filled him in on the details. He assured me he would pick up Jeffrey at nursery school and be home within fifteen minutes.

Three-quarters of an hour later, my family sat in the waiting room at the doctor's office. The nurse opened the door and with one glance at Aaron, ushered us in, only to bump into Dr. Kenefick in the main hallway. Placing his stethoscope on Aaron's heart, he listened carefully.

"Go into room two," he said to us. "Oxygen stat!" he yelled down the hall towards the nurses' office. He placed his hand on my shoulder, nudging me down the hall. "I'll be right in."

A nurse ran down the hall and into our room carrying a liter tank of oxygen. I was sitting on a chair with Aaron on my lap as she fixed the minuscule oxygen mask on Aaron's tiny face. When she finished, she placed the tank of oxygen on the floor next to me. Jerry and I quickly glanced at each other, fearing the possibilities. I could feel the pace and rhythm of Aaron's breathing against my abdomen, faint yet rapid at the same time.

I looked at Jerry again, as if I would find an answer on his face, finding only an agitating pain and fear that matched my own.

Hearing fast-paced footsteps coming down the hall, I pulled my eyes off Jerry and looked over at the door just as Dr. Kenefick walked in. The look in his eyes was totally serious, not the easy, fun-filled look that made his pediatric patients feel immediately comfortable with him.

"Your son is in congestive heart failure. He's got fluid in his lungs and around his heart," he said, soberly.

He opened up Aaron's undershirt and pointed at his sternum where we could see, quite obviously, the bottom piece of his sternum protruding from the pressure building up in his heart and lungs. I gasped, wondering how I had not noticed just how expanded his rib cage had become. His chest seemed about to explode from all the pressure building up behind the rib cage.

"I want you to go over to Stamford Hospital. I think it would be faster if you went by car. I just have to finish up with one patient and then I'll be over to meet you. Dr. Swidler, one of my partners, is doing rounds at the hospital. I'll call ahead to let him know you're coming in. He'll meet you in the emergency room. Go now. And keep the oxygen mask secured on Aaron's face."

Jerry and I both nodded a shaky "yes." This was all happening too quickly. I don't think I'd ever been so scared.

Chapter Five

✳

Driving to the hospital seemed an eternity, the long spans of silence between our words intruded upon by an agitating fear grabbing at our thoughts. An internal battle ensued in each of us, a battle in our minds and hearts; minds which desperately tried to decipher all that was happening and hearts begging for God's grace.

Once at the emergency room and announced, I was briskly escorted to where they would be running sundry tests on Aaron, while Jerry waited with Jeffrey who was to be picked up by his Aunt Barbara, Jerry's sister. I sat on a hospital bed, Aaron on my lap, still with the oxygen mask secured over his nose and mouth. A nurse took off all but Aaron's diaper and socks, leaving him wrapped in his blanket, and pasted five electrodes over his heart. Dr. Swidler came right over, introduced himself, and started running the EKG. Within minutes, two residents were by his side, to assist or observe him: which, exactly, I was not sure. Several yards of paper scratched with readings from the EKG leads traveled through Dr. Swidler's hands and on down to the floor. I awaited anxiously for an answer but the EKG showed nothing abnormal.

I held Aaron close, attempting to provide him some sort of security while the residents ran the test again. In the meantime, Dr. Swidler explained that the nurse would be putting an intravenous line into Aaron's arm so they could draw blood and also administer Lasix, a drug to remove the life-threatening fluid around Aaron's heart and lungs.

Aaron put up a good fight as the nurse tried to feed the IV line into Aaron's arm, yet as difficult as it was to slide the needle into his tiny veins, she succeeded after two or three attempts. It was all I could do to hold Aaron still, desperately trying to ease his pain and allay what I felt to be an all-consuming fear. This would not be the last time I would be watching my baby express such anger towards well-intentioned figures in white lab coats.

Once the IV line was in place, the nurse administered the Lasix and Dr. Swidler went back to look at the results from the second run of EKG tests. Many more yards of paper passed through his hands this time, revealing not the slightest in the way of a diagnostic clue.

The doctors were stumped to find a reason for Aaron's enlarged heart, nor did they understand why he developed fluid on his lungs, so they decided to attempt a diagnosis using ultrasound. I felt enormously hopeless, my baby's life so blatantly threatened by who knew what.

My heart burdened, I found myself privately whispering to Aaron through anguished tears. Soulful words these were; from where I received the strength to speak them, I know not. "Aaron, buddy, if you need to leave, I won't hold you back. I love you so dearly and I'd miss you — God, I'd really miss you. But if you need to go back to God, I'll understand. I love you so much, sweetheart, really I do."

Dr. Swidler put a conducting cream on the ultrasound rod and started moving it around on Aaron's chest while keeping a close eye on the monitor for what was for me, an apprehensive five minutes. "So far, we're not finding anything," Dr. Swidler said, interrupting my thoughts, "but we'll keep doing the ultrasound a little longer."

I was in somewhat of an altered state, having removed myself from the chaos of the room to a quiet and centered place within. I started to chant a barely audible but most beautiful, calming Indian mantra, knowing I had to maintain a peace inside for Aaron's sake. I remember being somewhat conscious of the doctors hearing me chanting, but I didn't care at all. I needed to be there, wholly, for Aaron, no matter what happened.

I had forgotten, but at this point was reminded by the feeling of fullness of Aaron's diaper, that the Lasix was working. In fact, the drug was so effective that in twenty minutes, Aaron had entirely saturated his size extra small diaper. A nurse came by with a new diaper, removing the old one to be weighed to measure just how much fluid was being excreted, in this way accounting for all fluid changes in Aaron's body.

Dr. Swidler was unable to uncover anything with the ultrasound and Aaron, thanks to the Lasix, was stabilized somewhat, so Aaron was sent up to the pediatric intensive care unit. I went out to give Jerry an update, and found him with his sister, Barbara, who had just arrived to take Jeffrey to his grandparents until we got things sorted out.

My sister-in-law was frantic. In comparison, I was trance-like, trying my best to be calm and optimistic. I remember consciously positioning myself to be centered, to trust, to see the perfection in all this, God's plan, and I certainly did not need anyone tampering with that position. My response came from many years of spiritual searching and personal development work, hard work that tided me through the breakup of my first marriage, teaching me perhaps the most valuable life mastery tools I'd yet learned. I had come to realize the power our minds have to create our experience in the world.

Jerry, on the other hand, looked shell-shocked. I guessed it was near impossible for him to be out in the waiting area, not knowing anything, his heart victim to his mind anticipating answers.

Report given to Barbara and Jerry, nervous questions asked of me, questions for which I had neither answers nor any energy on what was happening, hugs and kisses to an almost-three-year-old son who hadn't the vaguest idea; Jerry and I ran upstairs to the pediatric Intensive Care Unit.

What a sight Jerry and I beheld. Through the glass

partition, we saw our little Aaron, lying in a junior-size bed, naked with the exception of his diaper. He looked so vulnerable, the oxygen mask remaining over his nose and mouth, EKG leads on his chest, an IV in his right forearm, and a little tab taped to the big toe on his right foot. The tab was an oxygen sensor that kept track of his oxygen saturation point, how much oxygen his body was absorbing. A big monitor hung from the ceiling to his right, droning a repetitious beep... beep... beep.

Dr. Kenefick had arrived and walked towards us from behind. Adjacent to him was Dr. Swidler. Dr. Kenefick, always so competent, looked at us, compassion pouring from his eyes.

"You guys hanging in?" he asked, sensing our anxiety.

We nodded and shrugged, as if to say "what else could we do?" "What's going on, what's wrong?" I probed.

"We don't know. We can't find anything that would cause this. Right now, at least, Aaron's condition is stable with the Lasix."

"Well, what are you thinking is wrong?" Jerry pressed.

"It's not uncommon for children of this age to have congenital heart defects. And it's highly treatable. We just can't identify anything yet."

"Then what do we do?" I asked.

"We think you should go down to New York Hospital. They're the tops in diagnosing pediatric cardiac cases. The head of neonatal cardiology is a Dr. Snyder. I did my residency with him. I trust him implicitly."

Jerry and I looked long and hard at each other, our fear escalating. We had no experience with these matters. Conventional medicine, unlike holistic medicine, was not an area where we had personal contacts. We had to make a decision quickly, a decision for which we were totally unequipped.

"We tried to arrange for a helicopter to transport Aaron down to the city to avoid the construction on the FDR Drive. But they're saying the winds are too strong tonight, that it would be too risky."

The idea of my little Aaron flying in a helicopter caused an eerie tremor to course through my body. The only flying I wanted him to do at his age was in his dreams, with the blessed angels.

"An ambulance can leave in a little while. Lori, if you'd be more comfortable, you can travel in the ambulance with Aaron and let Jerry follow behind. Or, just meet him at the hospital. I assure you, Aaron will arrive safely."

I pictured the ride in the ambulance. Aaron would probably be in an incubator-size crib, secured by straps to the floor. There would be a bench along the wall that I feared would be narrow and therefore difficult to sit on securely. And then there was the road, the FDR Drive, with the reputation as the bumpiest highway in New York City, in perpetual repair for its famous potholes. Aaron was soundly sleeping for the first time all day and, I thought, might very well continue to sleep the whole ride. Would he even know if I was there?

"We have some paperwork to fill out, transfer

forms and such. Then we can release him. On second thought, I'm sure there are some things you both will need to take care of. You'll most likely need to be in the hospital for at least a few days. I suggest you go home, pack some clothes, and take care of whatever necessities you'll need to tend to over the next few days. Aaron's sleeping calmly now. I'm sure he'll be okay."

I felt guilty for what felt like abandonment. "I wonder if Aaron will know if I'm with him or not. I don't want him to wake up and not see me there."

"I'm sure he'll sleep through the trip, his body's been through an awful lot. It needs the rest, and thanks to the Lasix, he's finally comfortable enough to do just that." I appreciated Dr. Kenefick's reassurance, but I couldn't help picturing Aaron waking up and knowing I wasn't there with him. Dr. Kenefick must have been reading my mind because he reassured me once more that Aaron would be okay and that it would be best to go home with Jerry, manage whatever we needed to, and then drive to the city in comfort. I'm sure he meant my physical comfort. How could anyone expect mental comfort from me at this point?

Caught up in what to do, my mind was preoccupied with how to physically go about taking care of all that needed to be done. Who knew when we'd be coming home?

The doctors said their good-byes, Dr. Kenefick placing supportive hands on our shoulders before leaving us alone with Aaron.

I glanced over at Jerry. He was leaning over the side of the crib, looking at Aaron. Tears trickled down his cheeks. "Why my little Aaron? What did he ever do to deserve this? It's not fair. Why would you do this to my son, God, why?" Jerry's pain was unfathomable.

I don't know why, but at that moment, I was feeling strong. I embraced him from behind, attempting to soothe his aching heart.

We leaned over the crib together, looking at Aaron, both of us mumbling our love for this little one. We placed kisses on his tiny forehead and said a most loving goodbye which, unfortunately, was tainted by an unearthly fear. God, was it painful. Not fair, I thought, not at all fair.

I was sure my husband was taking the worst beating of his life, for never had I seen my strong hunk of a man looking so vulnerable. It scared me to see him like that, only magnifying my own vulnerability. As overwhelmed as I was, though, I felt I had to transform his fear while simultaneously dealing with my own, all to maintain the frame of mind I believed necessary to create the optimum environment to support Aaron's healing.

I wouldn't let on to Jerry. I needed to act strong. This was no time to let go and feel too vulnerable. Almost like machines, we set off to home to handle the unrelenting necessities.

Driving home, I lectured Jerry about how we needed to be strong for Aaron's sake. This was my keen intellect proselytizing what I believed in terms of spiritual truths, my heart desperately trying to shut out the agonizing pain. I'd been accustomed to mustering up stamina required to handle stress of an impersonal nature, like meeting deadlines for important projects, but never in my life had I experienced stress like this. By the time we got home, I had started freaking out, my mind jumping back and forth over all that had to be done. Nothing was fitting into the neat box of appearances I attempted at all cost to maintain. Everything seemed out of control. I realize now that I was so crazed because everything was out of my control, a core issue I've had to deal with in my own psychological and spiritual evolution, an issue my son's journey would propel me to resolve.

"Sweets, calm down," Jerry reassured. "Everything will get handled. Trust me. The doctors are taking care of everything. And Aaron's sleeping, finally. When we get home, we'll take care of everything, one thing at a time. It'll work out fine, you'll see." Pleased, I wondered where his newfound strength came from.

As I buried my face in the physical strength of the warm and padded crook of his neck, I cried my fear into his assurances.

The twenty-minute ride away from the bustling downtown to the quiet of our country street left me feeling grateful, a little bit more composed. Nervously, we put some clothes together and made phone calls. Our bodies moved on automatic pilot while our minds sorted through all the events of the past few weeks, trying to make some sense of it all, and on some level, even trying to make it all disappear. We passed each other as we went about taking care of things, afraid to look into each other's eyes for fear of having our own pain mirrored back. It didn't matter, though; we felt it in the ethers between us.

We left the house with a few days' worth of clothing,

some clothes and stuffed animals for Aaron, and even my running clothes. How I had the wherewithal to remember my running clothes, I'll never know.

Weary and hungry, our bodies winding down from the day, we landed at our favorite Chinese restaurant to pick up the take-out order we had placed before leaving home. Fishing for vegetables in a paper container, me with chopsticks and Jerry with a plastic fork, served as a great distraction for the drive down to Manhattan, dinner down the hatch with not enough time to get fully reinvested in our collective fears and concerns one more time around.

We were burned out emotionally. Over the course of this day, our minds had been filled to capacity with some of the most horrifying thoughts imaginable.

Chapter Six

✷

Stamford, although in an entirely different state, is a suburb of Manhattan, considered one of its bedroom communities, as so many of its residents commute daily into Manhattan to pursue highly stressful and sometimes prestigious careers. Jerry and I each grew up knowing Manhattan very well, as did most people who lived in any of the surrounding boroughs and the suburb of Long Island; Manhattan being the place everyone flocked to for the best in cultural entertainment. In addition, Manhattan boasts some well-known universities and medical schools, not to mention some very reputable medical centers offering state-of-the-art care.

New York Hospital was just one such medical center. One of its wings edged out over the FDR Drive, letting us know exactly where to exit the highway. Forty-five minutes after starting our Chinese food, with the view of the hospital in the distance, our apprehension escalated.

Off the ramp and onto local streets, we set to the

task of finding legal street parking, not an easy feat at ten in the evening after the residential population had bedded their cars for the night. Luckily, we found parking two blocks from the hospital, ran right over to the main entrance, and asked where we would find neonatal cardiology. The security officer standing duty, kind enough to call up to the unit to find out the status of Aaron's admission, informed us the ambulance hadn't yet arrived, and directed us to where Aaron would be, once admitted.

Ten minutes later, anxiously perched on a bench in a darkened waiting area right outside the neonatal unit, a nurse came out and informed us that in five minutes, once Aaron was set up, we would be able to see him. By this time, we were both aching to see our little angel, hoping he hadn't noticed our absence.

We were guided into the darkened unit. I noticed six cribs, most of which were empty. With the exception of the monitor's droning beeps, it was as quiet as a morgue, two lights hanging over the nurse's station, illuminating an area just large enough for the only other nurse on duty to keep current with the medical charts. My eyes swept through the entire unit, digesting any pertinent data in a few short seconds, and then I sighed in relief, having found Aaron tucked away in the corner cubicle.

Aaron was attached to monitors in much the same manner as in Stamford Hospital, with perhaps a better caliber of high-tech equipment. As Dr. Kenefick had suspected, Aaron was still sleeping, his body presumably bushed from the day's events.

I couldn't place my finger on it exactly, but Aaron looked different somehow, almost defenseless. Upon a more discerning inspection, I noticed cheeks so hollow and ribs so pronounced that I shivered at the sight of my precious one. He was looking absolutely emaciated. Then it dawned on me that this was the work of the Lasix. I kissed his forehead.

"How did things go in the ambulance?" Jerry asked the nurse.

"The medics said he slept the whole way," she replied. "He woke for a moment as we transferred him to the crib here and then he went right back to sleep." I sighed in relief as she walked away to complete some paperwork.

I looked around. The clock said eleven-ten. I confirmed five other cribs in the unit, only two filled. One-on-one nursing care for my son. I was glad it wasn't busy tonight. I went over to Jerry, to the security of his arms, my fear relentlessly encroaching any semblance of the peace of mind I attempted to maintain. I worried how this leg of our journey would unfold.

A distinguished-looking man came over to us, introducing himself as Dr. Snyder. Brainwashed to believe that the best doctors generally have poor bedside manners, I half expected a stuffy and impersonal presentation, especially at this renowned teaching institution. Much to my surprise, there was instant rapport with Dr. Snyder and I was calmed in his presence. I became hopeful he'd have our answer.

"Come with me across the ward so we can talk," he said. Jerry and I followed him to a rather bare conference room with lit panels on one of the walls. Several sheets of film were already clipped in place for Dr. Snyder's use. He reached into his pocket, withdrew a collapsible pointer, and moved it over the first square of film.

"I did ultrasound on your son's heart. Like the doctors at Stamford Hospital, I couldn't find anything wrong with him."

He paused through a deep inhale. My heart sunk.

He continued, "Once, and only once in my entire career have I ever seen what your son has."

A moment of relief; he knows what the enemy is.

"Something told me to take the ultrasound rod and scan through your son's fontanelle, you know, the soft spot on a baby's skull. That's when I picked it up."

It? What is it? The pointer moved down to the second sheet of film, only black and white with shades of gray in-between. All I could discern from the pointer's movements were fuzzy forms, as though I was looking through shadow-like concentric circles.

The pointer traced around the outermost circle. "This is the fontanelle."

Which of these fuzzy forms is the it?

"What your son has is an arterio-venous malformation at the vein of Galen, or for short, an AVM. It's between the third and fourth ventricle of the brain."

He paused. "Right there." The pointer moved onto a grayish sphere within the outermost ring, then onto the same grayish sphere in the next three quadrants of the film.

Dr. Snyder paused again, giving us a moment to digest the intricate information, I assumed, knowing full well it was somewhat foreign to us. I felt like someone had placed a vise grip on my throat. We now knew what the enemy was. I expected to feel relieved, but the fear only intensified, gripping more tightly around my throat.

"This A...V...M?" Jerry hesitated, questioning the terminology.

"Yes, AVM."

"What does this AVM do?" Jerry asked.

"In essence, it's a malformation of arteries in the brain. No one knows exactly why this happens. It's just a fluke of nature."

Great, I thought, I love substantial explanations. "Is it curable? I mean, where do we go from here? What do you do about it?" Frightened by this unexplainable entity, my voice started to quiver.

"You'll go to New York University Medical Center tomorrow morning. Aaron's in no immediate danger right now. A Dr. Berenstein is at NYU — he's a world-renowned specialist in this area. He works exclusively with children who have AVMs. I assure you, you'll be in the best hands."

Seemed like we'd heard something about renowned specialists earlier that same evening, but by now I wasn't sure of anything.

"Explain this a little more," Jerry said.

I was crushed. I didn't need to hear any more. It seemed an unbeatable enemy and I yearned to save my son from the onslaught. I walked out of the conference room, leaving Jerry and Dr. Snyder talking. I walked right over to the foot of Aaron's crib, innately knowing exactly where my soul needed to be.

The monitors droned on. Beep... beep... beep. Hypnotic, it transformed itself into black sound, a chorus to the noise in my battered psyche. Beaten and exasperated, I reached for the horizontal part of the crib's frame, the metal railing cooling my sweaty palms. Fearful, I dropped my forehead on the back of my hands, and finally let my tears fall, surrendering to the all-encompassing helplessness.

I was frozen in this position, crying for my son, for Jerry, and for myself. I knew not what God wanted and had no idea whether Aaron was to survive or not. The thought of his dying was sheer devastation. That thought numbing me and turning me to stone, short-circuiting my mind with static interference.

And then, all of a sudden, telepathically slicing right through that interference, came words from Aaron, words that were clear as day, not heard with volume, but nonetheless clear, most clear, heard as crystal clear thought. In my head, I heard Aaron's words, "Don't worry Mom. I'm going to be all right."

I lifted my face off the back of my hands. A most incredible peace infiltrated my devastation, transforming me into a state of flowing joyfulness. I knew. Yes, I knew as sure as I knew I had woken up that morning, no matter what the journey entailed, my son would be all right. He'd make it through. No words can do justice in describing the brilliant feeling bathing my soul in that moment. It was in the realm of Godly manifestations. I'm unshakably sure of it.

I stood there for several minutes, glowing from

the glory that claimed me, crying gently, completely beholden. Jerry walked up from behind me and embraced me, resting his head against my back. I could feel his devastation. I unraveled myself from his embrace and turned my face up towards his. If not my aura, then my face with its beaming smile collided with his state of mind, his energy field. He looked at me, querying an explanation for the disparity between our states of being.

Oddly, I didn't even think, not for a split second, that he would not believe what had just happened, what I had experienced.

"Don't worry, Jerry, Aaron's going to be okay. I know it. He told me. I heard him telepathically tell me, don't worry, Mom. I'm going to be all right."

Jerry yearned for my inner knowing to be his inner knowing. He wanted to believe what I said was true. Not that he questioned my credibility; this was not the first time circumstances out of the ordinary had happened to me. This experience hadn't happened to him personally, plain and simple; hence, it couldn't have the transformative effect on him that it had on me. But I knew it blessed him anyway. He hoped with a touch more confidence than he had had up until then. For me, it granted a firm inner knowing of what many people spend their entire lives seeking.

Chapter Seven

✳

To the best of my recollection, it was just after eleven P.M. Jerry and I were hovering over Aaron's crib, hoping he'd open his eyes for at least a few minutes. Full well knowing nothing could be done tonight, we opted to stay by his side, as if we expected something to happen.

Out of the corner of my eye, I caught Jerry acknowledging someone's entrance into the unit. Curiously, I turned around to see who he could possibly know here, only to discover two people, friends of ours, had somehow found our whereabouts.

"I can't believe it. Donny, Bill, how did you know we were here?" I questioned.

"Susan got a hold of me," he said, releasing himself from our warm embrace. "She told me something was wrong with Aaron and that you would be here. I don't know why, but I felt compelled to come out and see if I could help," he added, and then explained the slim chance that Susan could have found him in one of his offices as it was his day off. Donny was a big believer in synchronicity, believing in no accidents or coincidences, only perfection in all occurrences.

If ever there were a natural born leader, it would be Donny. Brilliant in every endeavor, he has a true gift for healing. Bill and his close friend and colleague, Scott, were studying an innovative form of chiropractic called network chiropractic, a technique Donny had developed. Rather than attempting spinal alignment using structural manipulations, a soft touch is applied to a series of points along the spine. This loosens the soft tissue, which due to physical, emotional, or chemical stress, has become taut, restricting the spine's agility. Working these key points allows the cerebrospinal fluid to circulate more freely, causing the tension on the spinal cord to be released, normalizing nerve function and promoting overall healing. Jerry and I had received chiropractic care from Donny and vouched for the comprehensive feeling of well-being and health we enjoyed. We also had seen Donny's work immensely facilitate healing for several of his patients who were fighting chronic disease processes.

"We're really grateful you both came," Jerry said.

"So this is your little baby," remarked Donny, walking towards Aaron's crib. "This is our little Aaron."

"So what's going on? Fill me in on everything." Donny was moving his hand in the air over Aaron's head, apparently looking to feel from Aaron's body just exactly what it suffered. "It feels like he's been through the mill."

"Aaron was in congestive heart failure, but at our local hospital, they couldn't figure out why. They treated him with Lasix, purely to treat the symptoms. But when we brought him here, the doctor somehow thought to move the ultrasound rod over Aaron's fontanelle, and that's when he picked up the malformation of arteries and veins which he referred to as an AVM. He said it's near the vein of Galen. At any rate, he looks so emaciated right now because the Lasix drained all the excess fluid from his body."

As I briefed them, Donny motioned Bill to the foot of Aaron's crib. Donny slid his hands under Aaron's head and placed his fingers at the base of Aaron's skull while Bill held the soles of Aaron's feet. Jerry and I watched in grateful silence.

While Donny worked, he spoke to us. "Aaron's nervous system is on total overload. I'll try to clear out as much as possible, but I'd really recommend calling me in the next day or so. His body needs more work. He's been through quite a lot. He'll be okay, though. It's obvious he's an old soul."

Old soul. I shuddered. The words marched up my spine and into my brain where they burned indelibly. I felt compelled to relate Aaron's communication to me. Knowing Donny, I knew he wouldn't think I was crazy.

"I'm not at all surprised," he said in response to my story. "In my opinion, it's absolutely necessary you both set up a prayer circle, around the clock, twenty-four hours a day for three days." He removed his hands from Aaron's body, as did Bill, taking his cue. The four of us gathered alongside Aaron's crib.

"My wife, Jackie, and I will take from twelve to two A.M.," he graciously offered.

"I'll take the three to four A.M. time slot," Bill piped in.

Jerry and I looked at them in near disbelief of their soulful offering. "You guys are too much," Jerry said, and went to embrace them.

"Come, both of you. Aaron's not the only one who's been through the mill today. I'll work on both of you too. Let's go find a place to sit down. It's time for you guys to take a break."

How could we turn down such an offer from Donny? Somewhat released from the hardship of the day, we kissed Aaron on the forehead and went out into the darkened hall to lie on a bench.

As strange as it may sound, by the time Donny finished working on us, I felt even more grateful. My son was lying in a crib attached to monitors checking almost every bodily function imaginable and I was in a state of complete ease and hopefulness, my mind flipping through the list of people we would soon call, asking to pray for Aaron.

Jerry glanced at his watch, announcing it was twelve-thirty. We all embraced, and then Jerry and I watched Donny and Bill leave. I looked over at Jerry. He looked lighter, less tense, kind of like he was beginning to surrender into the flow of things, just a bit. He took me in his arms.

"That was incredible," he said. "I can't believe Donny and Bill went out of their way to do that for us. Maybe everything will be okay."

"It will be, Sweets. We just have to hang on for the ride. Aaron will be fine."

We went back in to a still-sleeping Aaron to say our goodnights for the evening. Jerry and I were burned out, our emotional checking account overdrawn. We desperately needed to rest so we said our sweetnesses to Aaron, and as hard as it was, peeled ourselves away.

Once in the car, thriving on a second wind, I got into busy mode. We had but a twenty-minute ride to Jerry's parents in Queens and I was committed to compiling the prayer list we started in the hospital. Jerry got into it also, offering to call friends in Israel for whom our sleeping hours would be easily accommodated due to a six-hour time difference.

I was gratefully surprised at Jerry's actions. Even though we held identical spiritual beliefs, our outward expressions of those beliefs were quite different. Normally, I would take charge; I'm sure Aaron's need inspired Jerry to reach beyond his comfort zone, to be less subtle than usual, even a little proactive. I was most glad for the company in this endeavor, that was for sure.

We pulled up to Jerry's parent's apartment complex, finding parking behind the building. After trudging up four flights of stairs, we opened the door of the apartment, filed straight into the guest bedroom, and fell right into bed. I'm sure I was fast asleep in under three minutes.

Chapter Eight

✳

I awakened very early the following morning, before anyone, or the sun for that matter, was up, and went out for my daily run. Upon my return, I found my in-laws, Jenny and Norman, and Jerry talking in the living room; my son Jeffrey was still fast asleep. Unlike many of their senior friends, Jenny and Norman were both energetic and still actively involved in their own life pursuits. Norman was retired and extremely involved in his new hobby and friend, his computer. His days revolved around becoming computer literate and chauffeuring his wife to and from school; Jenny insisting on continuing to work as a teacher in a local school to assure herself of the pension she had worked many years to obtain. In between the computer and teaching, they both did Israeli dancing once a week, my mother-in-law adding a bi-weekly exercise class.

As I stepped into the apartment, my in-laws came over to me and doled out compassionate hugs. "You guys must really love me to hug me all sweaty like this," I joked.

My father-in-law laughed at my remark and immediately began to offer me assistance, as though I had just finished a marathon. "Come. You must be exhausted. Sit down and rest."

"I'm okay, Dad."

"Forgive me. I'm to be corrected. I forget that you're the one who always feels better after a run, not exhausted like most people." I knew what he was referring to. Jerry and I had spent our honeymoon cycling through Europe for a month and had landed back in New York about five in the morning. The journey home was like a suspense-filled Agatha Christie story, a sleepless eighteen-hour ordeal involving an all-night train ride from the South of France to Brussels, Belgium, halted mysteriously for three hours. (We later found out this was because some troubled person threw himself on the tracks in front of the train.) The trip ended in a mad dash to the plane for New York, with two bicycles in tow. By the time we arrived in New York, I needed something to jar me back into my body, and running is precisely the thing which does that. My father-in-law, kind enough to meet us at the airport, thought I was absolutely crazy, but when he saw how I looked when I came back from my run, understood me fully. In fact, he oftentimes reminds me of this incident, me chuckling inside for it is one fanaticism of mine that he has some appreciation for; perhaps the only.

"Actually," I said, wiping the sweat from my brow, "what I need is some water." Even though it was just after 6:30 when I went for my run, it was already up to 75 degrees and quite humid. "I'll be right back."

I went to the kitchen to get our Thermos of filtered water, swiveled the top open, and gulped down some water as I walked back out to the living room. I paused right by Jerry's chair and asked him, "How are you doing?"

"Hanging in," he said.

"Jerry told us everything. You don't have to worry one bit about what to do with Jeffrey. We'll keep him here while you're at NYU. His grandfather will love it." Jenny paused, fighting back some tears. "I just wish it were for other reasons." The tears succeeded despite her resistance to them, and trickled on down her sallow cheeks.

During my run, I had been wondering how my mother-in-law would handle this. She'd had enough of her own tsouris (Yiddish for troubles) in life, one being the loss of a son at age forty to a major coronary. This mother of four had many a sleepless night. Jenny was of strong fiber, bearing up well under pressure, but I could tell that inside, the pain ate at her. I have a lot of love and respect for my mother-in-law. She shoots straight from the hip, no hidden agendas with this woman, no manipulation. What you see is what you get.

I sat next to her, placing my arm around her. "Aaron is going to be okay. I know it in my heart, Mom. Just say a prayer for him, all right?"

She put her head on my shoulder. "I've been praying all night."

"Actually, I figured you would. You're good like that." Only heartfelt expressions from this matron. I stroked her hair, gave her a squeeze and then turned to Jerry, reminded of our prayer circle. "We have to make some phone calls this morning to set up the prayer circle."

"You underestimate me, Sweets. I have all but two of the time slots filled."

"What? When did you do that?" I was tickled beyond belief.

He smiled at me, obviously pleased with himself. "When you wiped out last night, I got up and called Israel and got Schulie and Abie to take the early morning slots. Then, this morning, just after you left for your run, I got up and called down the list of people we made last night. I have to tell you, I'm totally blown away by the amount of love our friends are sending our way."

I could see by the look in his eyes just how filled with love he really was. In our day-to-day lives, we never have to ask friends for things like this, and in fact, it had never even dawned on us that we'd ever have to. How much we take for granted. One thing this experience would beat into me is gratitude, big time. Living in gratitude for even the seemingly insignificant or apparent negative in my life.

"What's this prayer stuff?" Jerry's dad asked. "What this baby of yours needs is medical attention." Count on Dad to attempt bringing us back down to earth, to real life, to practicality. Every family needs a loving, staunch realist and Dad was the one to play that role. He's one of those people who has to see it to believe it. The beliefs Jerry and I held were much too esoteric for him, some of the decisions we had made, totally offending, like choosing not to perform the ceremonial circumcision on our sons. When Jeffrey was born, Dad didn't talk to us, let alone hold his first grandson, for eleven months. There were consequences for one's actions in life, and he often thought it his responsibility to dole them out. As angry and frustrated as we were at times, Jerry and I expressed our love for him, choosing to see Dad's love shouting out in the wake of his actions.

Not wanting to get into an irritating philosophical debate first thing in the morning, I quickly drew upon skills learned in a communication course I had taken years ago.

Validate. That was the operational word here.

"That too, Dad. Calm down. We're not going to deprive Aaron of medical attention. I promise you." Fighting my own intolerance, I looked him square in the face, stifling the urge to become uncontrollably emotional, like a woman with intense PMS, and matter-of-factly added, "But you do know that prayer can go a long way as well."

Avoiding a retort, I quickly turned to Jerry. "I think I'll shower so we can get to the hospital before the doctor does."

"Take your time," Jerry replied. "I called the hospital just before you came back from your run. Aaron slept through the night with no difficulties. Everything is stable and they're feeding him through one of those feeding tubes."

"When are they transferring him to NYU?" I asked.

"There's a bed waiting for him. They expect he'll be admitted around ten A.M. and requested we just go straight over there to simplify the transfer."

As Jerry spoke, a sleepy Jeffrey poked his head around the bend from the foyer into the living room. "Mommy! Daddy!" He did a bee-line to my lap, jumped into it, wrapped his skinny arms around my neck and planted a kiss on my lips. "You're all sweaty, Mommy."

Sweaty or not, I held him tight, grateful, in a way I'd never been before, for his dear presence in my life. "I know, Sweetheart. Mommy got up real early and went out for a run," I said, finishing off my hug and kiss in response to his. "Go give Daddy a hug and kiss too. He's not sweaty like I am."

"Where's Aaron, Mommy? Is he okay?" I pulled him back, close to my bosom, resting his head in the crook of my arm. I loved holding Jeffrey in my arms like this. He was so delicate, such fine features defined his face, grown-up features, from the time he was born. My clone, facially and behaviorally. My mother swore him on me my whole childhood; whenever she had challenges with me, when my tenacity got a hold of her. "I hope you have one just like yourself," she'd say, unleashing her frustrated anger.

Jerry and I glanced at one another, knowing this moment had to come, but not talking in any length about what we would tell Jeffrey.

"Aaron's in the hospital, Sweetheart," I responded. "He's sick. But in the hospital, there are many doctors who can help him feel better."

"I'm going to work on the computer with Grandpa while you're in the hospital with Aaron." It was obvious that my in-laws had already answered some of his concerns. Then he jumped off my lap and onto Jerry's, and I slipped away to take my shower.

I seemed to move back and forth between feeling okay, kind of empowered, and mostly hopeless. These moods just moved into my space, intruding on the self-talk of my analytical mind. How were we going to explain all this to Jeffrey? How were we going to be able to care for his very important emotional needs while staying with Aaron in the hospital? These thoughts plagued my mind, me feeling the weight of this responsibility, I assumed, much like any other mother would.

Chapter Nine

✳

A short hour later, we met Aaron at NYU Medical Center. NYU is a large teaching institution, renowned for its neurosurgery, cardiovascular, and pediatric services. Right smack at the base of midtown, it boasts a location with easy access to a nicely landscaped two-mile-long promenade with phenomenal views of the East River and its bridges, a wide diversity of restaurants, and very decent shopping, all of which were some of the better features of what would become our off-and-on New York City abode over the next eight months.

Through the Venetian blinds, the morning sun streamed, its strength producing an annoying glare and adding heat to an already much-too-hot room. Aaron shared the room with another baby around two years old who got to sleep in a crib, Aaron himself in an incubator. Accustomed to generally seeing only premature babies in such contraptions, I shuddered when I saw him through the plastic dome. There were two holes along the length of the incubator through which we could place our arms to have physical contact with Aaron's frail body, that being the extent to which we could tactilely experience one another. And he was not to be in either of our arms for at least the next twenty-four hours, a time during which we craved to nourish him with every bit of love we could provide.

We must have answered the same sundry questions from well-meaning nurses and residents at least a half-dozen times during the first few hours of our stay. I couldn't care less about the questions after the first few rounds; my only desire was to take Aaron out of the incubator and nurse him, his hungry cries piercing straight through me. He kept looking over at me, his eyes speaking what I interpreted to be a yearning for the consolation of my manna. Unlike yesterday, he was very alert and expressive, and in a way, this was more painful in that there was no way I would be able to meet his nursing needs. One of the well-meaning nurses gave me a pacifier, but I knew my son better. He wanted the real thing. Nonetheless, I had to try as he was not allowed to nurse; and much to my surprise, this being the first time he ever sucked a pacifier, he did fairly well. Jerry and I took turns, hunched over the incubator, our hands poised to pop it back in his mouth every time it popped out, which was frequent at this point in his learning curve.

It was quite a few hours of popping pacifiers later that we finally got to meet someone from Dr. Berenstein's team. In fact, it was close to seven P.M. when one of his surgical residents came by. Thankfully, Aaron was sleeping soundly. After explaining that Dr. Berenstein was finishing a procedure, he launched into a quite comprehensive description of the work that would be done to close off some of the malformed arteries in Aaron's head.

"We have scheduled Aaron for the day after tomorrow, at which time Dr. Berenstein will perform this most delicate procedure. By using angiography, he will first ascertain precisely where each and every one of the malformed arteries is."

Angiography. My mind searched its memory banks to retrieve descriptive information. I'd certainly heard of angiography before, however, most often in respect to cardiovascular surgery. Radioactive dye is injected into a person's bloodstream, and a catheter with a microscopic scope at the end of it is snaked from a vein in the groin through the circulatory system to whatever location is of concern. The radioactive dye enables the radiologist to direct the catheter and see occlusions, or in Aaron's case, specifically, how the malformed blood vessels were laid out.

The resident continued, "Then he'll insert a smaller catheter through the larger one to position surgical crazy glue to close off the malformed arteries."

"Crazy glue?" Jerry and I chimed in. Visualizing crazy glue, its composition and normal use, made it very difficult for me to imagine this stuff in the human body. "It's a surgical crazy glue, not the commercial glue, that will be placed strategically to shut down the flow of blood through the malformed arteries."

That clarified things a little bit, at least. It probably had some different properties than the stuff that comes in the green cylinder that makes your fingers stick together if you're clumsy with it. Still, never in a million years would I have ever conceived of such a complicated and intricate procedure.

After having a multitude of questions fired at him, he politely informed us we would be meeting Dr. Berenstein the following morning and that we were best to digest all he was telling us so we could organize our thoughts and ask more pointed questions of Dr. Berenstein himself. And so he left us, with an array of vivid images to sort through, images which would prance in front of our eyes throughout the night, haunting our much-needed sleep.

As for where parents with extremely ill children get that much-needed sleep in a major city hospital...Jerry had done some snooping around and found out through the parent grapevine that the brown Naugahyde padded chair in our room expanded into a bed of sorts. By reclining the back of the chair parallel to the ground and then pulling out a third panel from underneath the seat, much like the way a trundle bed pulls out, we were able to transform the already cheaply padded chair into what we thought would be, at best, a cheaply padded bed. Since the bed was barely wide enough for one person, Jerry opted to sleep on the couch in the parents' room just down the hall.

With great reservation and gratitude all at the same time — after all, I was going to be able to sleep arm's distance from my son — I tried out the bed. Awful, absolutely awful. It was worse than a cheap fold away cot, surface-wise and width-wise. With my shoulders being framed by what were once unpadded wooden chair arms, I considered moving to the floor. An infinitely more appealing option, but against hospital regulations... or so a nurse informed me. To put it mildly, I felt like I was caged in, but not nearly as restricted as I was to feel later on.

Nighttime eventually came. Some kindly nurse's aide bestowed upon me the gifts of a pillow, a sheet, and a blanket. I wondered from where she confiscated it; that is, until Jerry showed up with his own. How in the world did he find out where the linen closet was? Trust my husband to roam around, meet people, and gather information on the ins-and-outs and politics of surviving the big city hospital. Jerry, with his own sheet and blanket, kissed me goodnight, and went down to the parents' room. I kissed Aaron goodnight and lay down. The noise in the hall had reduced itself to a dull roar, some mothers pushing strollers, attempting to lull their restless children to sleep, a ritual I would see for many a night to come.

My thoughts were filled with pictures of catheters snaking through the arteries in Aaron's body. Just as I nodded off, I felt hands gently shaking me back to reality, Jerry informing me there were no free beds in the parents' room. All were taken by parents who had children in intensive care.

And that was how my uncomfortably narrow bed was to become even narrower, both of us lying on our left sides like spoons neatly laid out on the traditional red-and-white-checkered picnic tablecloth, snug and tight to consolidate space. How we ever managed to fall off to sleep I'll never know. And to stay asleep, we spooned right, spooned head to foot; we tried every spooning position imaginable. Staying asleep for more than three-quarters of an hour was a small miracle in itself. This was but one of the many things I found myself laughing about and being grateful for in this time of crisis. I call it perspective.

Chapter Ten

✳

Our wake-up call came from none other than Dr. Berenstein at seven the following morning. The unassuming doctor boasted a tired appearance, dressed in his dingy green surgical clothes. We did not think him to be of this country — broad and rounded facial features marked his tired face which was framed with tousled dirty-blonde hair. A short man, no more than five and a half feet, and the totality of his appearance in no way matched his Jewish name. As the words "good morning" came forth from his mouth, I noted a faint Spanish accent that only accentuated the apparent inconsistency. Later, we discovered he was of Mexican Jewish heritage.

In a hasty manner, he introduced himself. His every movement was energized with vitality and excitement for his work, as distinct from what most would perceive as impatience. At his side stood three of his young surgical residents, each one looking more fatigued than the next. As they spoke, their accents revealed their nationalities: French, English, and the resident from last night, Avi, Israeli. Avi, lanky and tall, seemed to tower two feet over Dr. Berenstein, the sum total of their energies, imposing, as they hovered around Aaron, examining him and asking questions of Jerry and me. In these short few moments, I was to understand Dr. Berenstein's magnitude.

"I am told Avi informed you of the nature of the procedure we will perform tomorrow," Dr. Berenstein offered. "Do you have any questions?"

As we were still wiping the sand from our eyes, caught somewhat off-guard by the entourage, we didn't. "Right now, we don't," Jerry said. We're still digesting the information we were given last night."

"I'll be back later this evening, after we're done with the three procedures we've got scheduled today. We'll talk then," he finished, and then motioned his residents to follow him out. Their visit lasted a brief ten minutes and left us a bit stunned. We let it go, figuring it wiser to gather our thoughts and present our questions later.

Throughout the day, Jerry and I hashed out everything, compiling questions about this never-before-heard-of procedure. The ever-present veil of fear and concern weighed heavily, the only calm coming from the fact Aaron would be treated by the most experienced pair of hands this side of the Atlantic.

Later came. About thirteen hours later. Dr. Berenstein appeared at our door and at the offer of a chair, I collapsed into it, totally worn from the day's events. Aaron was sleeping, and Jerry and I were indulging in take-out salads from the Oriental market.

"That looks good," Dr. Berenstein said. I surmised

he was very hungry, hoping his wife was keeping dinner warm.

"Would you like some?" Jerry asked.

"Thanks, but I'll eat when I'm done with rounds." I couldn't help but raise my eyebrows in disbelief — thirteen hours of surgery and he still had rounds to do.

"I don't need to tell you your child has an extremely rare condition," he began. "We don't know why this happens, so first of all, don't blame yourselves." He was looking straight at me, yet the thought of blaming myself occurred to me only once, and fleetingly, at that.

"Tomorrow, I will be able to see exactly what's going on, specifically, how many and where these malformed arteries lie. I hope to close off as many as possible, hopefully all, in fact. Your son is the only procedure I've got scheduled for tomorrow. We'll start with him around seven in the morning; however, I don't know when we'll finish. The nurses on your unit will be kept apprised by our nurses throughout the day. That's how you'll know what's going on."

The enormousness of what would transpire tomorrow filled me; I could only be grateful for having Aaron in the hands of this incredibly talented individual.

Jerry asked a few simple questions, purely to solidify in his mind the procedure that we hoped would get Aaron's life out of danger. Patient and caring, Dr. Berenstein went over everything. I felt all I should do was hand it up to the Higher Power. I'd accepted our position, the circumstance extraordinarily challenging, but ours to contend with nonetheless. We were aware of having but one option, and he was sitting right in front of us. We trusted this man with our child's life — to us, he was a Godsend.

Chapter Eleven

✳

Jerry and I rose with the sun the following morning to a gray city, the clouds of evening past not yet burned off by a blazing summer sun, just beginning its dutiful march towards the horizon.

A nurse came in at six-forty-five, informing us that Aaron was expected in the operating room and that we were to leave in five minutes. Jerry and I threw our sweats on, apprehension skyrocketing. The nurse came back with a junior stretcher, and transferred a still-sleeping Aaron onto it after disconnecting him from all the monitors and sealing off the IV's. She hung a tank of oxygen from an IV pole which Jerry pushed alongside the stretcher onto the elevator.

We arrived on the second floor and were escorted past a large nurse's station to a waiting area. I picked up Aaron per the nurse's direction. "Good luck," she said. "I'm sure everything will turn out well. They'll call for you when the operating room is ready."

We paced back and forth, side by side, to keep the IV pole in tow. It seemed a long while before we were called, long enough for a sun to erase dawn's shadows on the medical complex's sky-scraping buildings. Very few words passed between me and Jerry, mostly heartfelt gazes doted on Aaron during our morning shuffling.

Meanwhile, in the operating room, two nurses moved in tandem, setting up shiny instruments for the doctors while the anesthesiologist, a graying man in his fifties, carefully checked his instruments.

We were escorted into the room by one of the nurses, the operating table, monitors, an observatory area, all coming into plain view. Classical music graced the room, ever so slightly soothing my jitters with its playfulness.

The anesthesiologist introduced himself. "Please place your son right here," he said, motioning with his hand as it tapped on the operating table. He removed Aaron's oxygen mask and replaced it with another mask with tubes running from one of his machines.

"Your son will feel no pain, I promise," he said. "This is just to get him sleepy. The anesthesia will be administered through an IV line once he is asleep, and I will monitor it on this machine, right over here." Frankly, my attention was focused to a greater extent on the separation anxiety I was feeling.

We lingered for a half minute longer, until the anesthesiologist suggested we leave. "Go for a cup of coffee or something. You've got a long day in front of you. We'll keep the nurse on your unit informed," he assured us.

We each kissed Aaron good-bye and stepped backwards out of the room, savoring every last look at Aaron. Then, we walked back to the elevator, arms around one another, heads hung low. The void was immense.

It took one and a half hours to set up the intravenous lines and prep Aaron for the procedure, his three surgical residents checking on Aaron periodically. At nine A.M., Dr. Berenstein walked into the operating room gulping down strong, black coffee tempered by two packets of Sweet'N Low. Almost on cue, he tossed the Styrofoam cup into the garbage, held up his hands, and was fitted with snug surgical gloves. His mind was focused on this helpless child and the enormousness of the task ahead. Of the over two hundred cases ever diagnosed, Dr. Berenstein had treated over half these infants, with another doctor in France treating most of the rest. Well-seasoned and confident, he was certainly the right man for the job.

His surgical team was ready for him: two nurses, his surgical residents, and the anesthesiologist all fully reviewed and prepared for the many-staged progression which could fill their day. Although quite experienced in this unique and most delicate procedure, this particularly rare anomaly was new to them.

The CAT scan performed by Dr. Berenstein's X-ray staff was clipped to a lit panel on the wall in front of him. He had studied these pictures, fully aware this externally sourced picture provided a less specific image than angiography, which would grant him the exacting clarity he required.

Prior to Dr. Berenstein's entry, the anesthesiologist had catheterized the right femoral artery with what is called a four French Introducer catheter. Dr. Berenstein inspected it, for through this starting point, he would negotiate his Tracker microcatheter for angiographic study and eventual embolization of the malformed arteries.

With flawless focus, Dr. Berenstein placed the microcatheter through the Introducer catheter and gently maneuvered it towards Aaron's head and up the left vertebral artery. Feeling some resistance, he nudged the catheter ever so gently several times and then informed his team, "I can't catheterize the distal portion of the vertebral artery. I'm going to attempt an approach through the carotid artery system."

Not an uncommon barrier, he thought, as he backed the catheter down the vertebral artery. After all, the blood vessels in these infants are almost microscopic.

He now began his ascent up the left carotid artery, visualizing exactly where he'd need to go from here to track into the conglomeration of arteries he planned to close. But again, he was stopped, unable to progress a millimeter further.

He glanced at the anesthesiologist, who perpetually kept in check precisely how much anesthesia Aaron was given. All was in check on his part. The monitors on Aaron's heart and respiration rate showed that those readings were also in check. A nurse wiped the sweat from his brow. Again, he gently slid the catheter down with the intention of tracking up the right internal carotid artery next.

Successfully entering this artery, he breathed a deep sigh of relief. It was now ten-thirty-seven. Gently again, he wiggled the microcatheter on into the cavernous carotid, but could not advance it any further. Dissatisfied, he removed the entire microcatheter assembly system and next introduced a Magic microcatheter with a 0 calibrated leak balloon, a narrower and more flexible catheter with the additional quality of a balloon attachment.

This time, he chose to track up his original choice of entry, the left vertebral artery. It was almost noon, he must have thought, as he took a deep breath again, then visualized his course, and delicately maneuvered the new catheter along its route. Minutes passed, the weaving of this catheter slightly more difficult than the first, the goal, even more distal, the posterolateral choroidal artery.

"I'm in it. I've catheterized the distal portion of the posterolateral choroidal artery. Give me a frontal and lateral to examine my position." Radio-opaque dye rushed through Aaron's arteries as a multitude of pictures were taken by one of the nurses. An extremely proficient crew, he was grateful for their assistance.

All looking on were stunned. Revealed was a complex vascular malformation which showed marked redundance, a multitude of unnecessary replication of the choroidal arterial system in which the catheter presently was. In addition, there was a significant fistula, or dilation, in the medial vein of prosencephaly; by definition, a particular vein in the front of the brain, also named the vein of Galen after the person who discovered it. The result of this fistula was an abnormally unrestricted flow into the next group of vessels: namely, the falcine sinus, confluent sinus and jugular venous system. What was revealed here was a direct flow from arteries to veins, with none of the slowing of blood flow enabled by capillaries normally connecting arteries to veins. Dr. Berenstein hadn't seen such a complex malformation in quite a long time. It was amazing that this child survived birth and lived without artificial support until just two days ago.

The malformation extended further. Deep into the venous system, it weaved its havoc-causing web. Even more abnormal drainage was found exiting the cerebral aspect of the brain, a vein called the Basal Vein of Rosenthal. As the dye recirculated, more malformations were noted, significant arteries feeding directly back into this area. Phenomenally complex, it would take more than this single procedure to correct the intricate malformation.

Considering Aaron's weight, the time (inching towards one o'clock), and the need to limit the amount of dye circulating through his just about six pounds, Dr. Berenstein decided to start treatment. This child, he thought, would provide extraordinary learning material for his next case study.

Avi prepared the all-important mixture, which consisted of 80% surgical crazy glue, technically called NBCA mixture, and 20% Pantpaque, the radioactive-opaque dye which allows for a visual display of the exact placement of the NBCA.

Dr. Berenstein, with painstaking accuracy, injected a very small amount of the mixture into the posterior lateral choroidal artery, and occlusion of this vessel as it bifurcates was obtained however, further distal penetration was not possible. Feeling somewhat pressured, he had another of his surgical residents remove the catheter assembly system while he himself took a short break to reassess the situation. There were many parameters requiring his consideration, precise observations and measurements from which life-saving decisions needed to be made.

Dr. Berenstein decided to advance yet another microcatheter to the medial left aspect of this complex and, after numerous attempts, succeeded in catheterizing this branch of vessels. Quickly, more dye was injected to ensure correct placement of the next batch of NBCA. Time was marching on without a halt, Aaron under anesthesia for almost eight hours, the dye coursing through his system almost to the limit allowable. It was three-thirty in the afternoon and all were becoming somewhat weary from the exacting work of the day.

Avi again prepared a small mixture of the NBCA, which was successfully injected and seen to produce excellent occlusion of this area of the malformation. "The pictures never lie," Dr. Berenstein remarked, proud of his accomplishment. It was nearing time to wind down, so he asked for additional pictures to check on the embolizations performed and to size up exactly what was left to close off in the future.

Not so much as for the doctors, but arduous nonetheless, our day dragged. Somewhere around twelve noon, my parents arrived with their much-needed support. Today was one day I wasn't going out for my run, so instead, to burn off the nervous jitters, I bounded up and down the nine flights of stairs several times throughout the day.

By three-thirty, I collapsed onto the couch next to Jerry with a cup of herbal tea my thoughtful parents bought. There we stayed, Jerry and I looking across the room at my parents and out the window at the setting sun, numb and exhausted from the torture of the emotions plaguing our minds.

Chapter Twelve

✳

Holding several pieces of film under his arm, an obviously successful Dr. Berenstein walked into the parents' waiting room shortly after five-thirty. Briskly, as was his manner, he announced, "Aaron's okay. He's doing very well. He's alert and resting in the recovery room. We finished just a few minutes ago and successfully closed off six of the malformed arteries."

Anxious to hear more, my parents, Jerry, and I edged forward towards Dr. Berenstein. Noticing that my parents were interested, he asked, "Are these the baby's grandparents?"

"These are my parents. Sheila and Charles Schneider, Dr. Berenstein." My father and Dr. Berenstein shook hands.

"Let's go into one of the conference rooms so I can show you exactly what we accomplished today. Grandma and Grandpa, you're welcome to come."

My father threw me a glance. I suspected an awkwardness, as if he did not want to intrude, but I motioned him to join us, and out of the room we marched, following Dr. Berenstein down the corridor to a conference room.

I was surprised as we entered the room, for it was small and messy, chairs scattered around such that we had to divvy them out. We scurried about to settle in, ending up around a table in front of a lit x-ray panel onto which Dr. Berenstein was clipping his film. The lines of stress etched into his face told of the struggle he encountered doing this procedure on three-week-old babies.

He explained what was achieved. "As I told you, we were successful in closing off six arteries. From the radiological studies performed, we ascertained another six that we'll need to close at a later date. I am sure the work we accomplished today will get Aaron out of danger and allow him to start thriving."

He pointed at the film. On the black background were white squiggly lines, blood vessels appearing almost like a web of unraveled yarn, laid out in a design with no rhyme or reason. "These are the malformed arteries. It took an enormous amount of exacting work to sort them out."

My heart skipped a beat. How could development go awry and produce something as bizarre, as life-threatening, as this?

"Normally, arteries lead to smaller vessels called arterioles, which lead to even smaller vessels called capillaries. The resistance provided by these smaller vessels slows the flow of blood. These capillaries, in turn, become venuoles, which then become veins. In Aaron's brain, in the malformation, the arteries lead straight into veins. There are no capillaries to slow the velocity of the blood. Hence, the reason for Aaron's congestive heart failure. Blood pumped so quickly down into his heart that his heart couldn't handle the overflow."

That sinking feeling revisited my body. At that moment, I couldn't help but consider it a miracle that Aaron ever survived.

"Did you have any sonograms done during pregnancy?" Dr. Berenstein asked.

"No, I didn't. We didn't want any interventions, we wanted to do things naturally."

He sighed. "I remember now. You birthed your son at home. The nurses told me."

"We had a certified nurse midwife there to help," I said, attempting to hide my defensiveness. At that moment, I did not want to get into a philosophical discussion. Jerry and I decided to bring both our children into this world in ways no mainstream doctor would ever understand. My vulnerability meter was nearing the red lines.

"This is your daughter?" he asked my parents. I sensed a judgment about to come down on me.

My mother, true to form, replied, "We were not in support of their giving birth to this baby at home." My mother could win an award for consistently holding the accountable responsible for their actions. Especially me. At this point in time, I was needful of her support, not her judgment, and I could feel, welling up inside me, the old familiar anger of childhood. Jerry put his hand on my knee, knowing from experience how my insides churned when my mother got like this.

Thankfully, Dr. Berenstein wasn't really interested in beating on Jerry and me. "Sometimes, this can be picked up on sonogram. That was the only reason I asked. You are not responsible for this. Remember."

Despite my denial, on some level, I must have felt responsible. After all, Aaron grew in my body. My body which only I nourished and exercised daily. Dr. Berenstein's words cut right through my disparaging self-talk.

"Right now, your job is to fatten up this baby. We will need to do another procedure on him when he is three- or four-months-old. He's to eat fattening foods, French fries, ice cream! No raw vegetable plates. You are not to feed your baby like you feed yourself."

The thought of greasy French fries! I almost gagged. And how did he know I survived hospital food by ordering a raw vegetable plate at mealtime?

"No vegetarianism for Aaron, Lori. You heard what the doctor said," my father, the carnivore, sung out.

My blood was quickly approaching 212 degrees Fahrenheit. It was unlike my father to join my mother on the fighting front. Under my breath, I said, "Jerry, right now, I want to kick out both of them. They've no right to talk to me like this." I was holding back a reservoir of tears, on the verge of overflowing.

"I'll handle it," he whispered back. Then, with protective authority, he claimed, "This is not the time, Mom and Dad. What we need now is your support, not your opinions."

Dr. Berenstein, sensing the tension in the air, attempted to temper things a bit. "Listen, all I'm saying is that it's hard for me to snake catheters through limbs tiny as chicken legs. I need to know you're going to fatten him up, so it's easier to get into his veins next time." Then his tone softened, his coronary muscle exercising itself. "You know, I lose a piece of my heart each and every time I work on one of these kids. Now, go. Go downstairs to the recovery room and see your little angel. We'll talk another time."

His words about losing a piece of his heart anchored their way into my heart, revealing to me just a fragment of the soft human side of his professional persona, a fragility he needed to keep under cuff.

Chapter Thirteen

*

We high-tailed out of that conference room and bounded down seven full flights of stairs, wonderfully ecstatic. Before entering the recovery room, we donned paper gowns, I assumed to assist in keeping the area sanitary. A nurse brought us over to Aaron, whom we found quite alert and responsive. He was a different child. Content and obviously comfortable for the first time in his short life, he looked at me. I wanted to take him into my arms and smother him with kisses, then nurse him. How I longed to have him at my breast, to reestablish our most intimate bond.

Jerry and I both were crying, purging the buildup from all the stress. Overwhelming gratitude rested in our hearts, and the more we reflected on what we had just been through, the more it expanded.

Another nurse came over to inform us they were planning to bring Aaron to the pediatric intensive care unit, and that we should go upstairs and meet him there. Much easier to kiss Aaron good-bye this time, we obediently followed her direction.

Expectantly, we paced the halls. It was taking too long for this impatient mother and father, but thankfully we chatted with a few parents and a couple of nurses, informing them of Aaron's status. We'd only been in this hospital for three days, yet, in that time, we had bonded with a few fellow parents, seeking and giving support with an empathy, the likes of which I'd never seen.

A good half-hour later, and annoyed about it, we were allowed into the ICU. Little Aaron had a beautiful view overlooking the Fifty-Ninth Street Bridge. Still wide-awake and happy, I lifted him from the crib, cradling him in my arms. All was perfect in the world.

I was to have my first encounter with the establishment within the hour. The floor pediatrician came over to our cubicle and explained the protocol we would use to put the much-needed weight on Aaron's body. Because Aaron was not yet strong enough to suck, a nasal gastric (NG) tube would be placed through his nose and fed into the stomach to supply nutrition. And of course I would not be pleased with their choice of food: formula. I had been expressing milk for the three days that we had been in this hospital, and I was determined to have the doctor allow Aaron to benefit from it. Much to my surprise, he agreed, but he forbade me to nurse Aaron because they needed to keep track of everything going into his body. The whole ordeal had put a damper on my milk production and Aaron required supplementation. My next argument was for goat's milk, based on scientific research, which showed it to be the most like mother's milk, and far superior to cow's milk. Much to my surprise, the pediatrician agreed with me, but trying to find raw goat's milk in the city proved to be unfruitful, so pasteurized containers of goat's milk it was. I fought hard, though, calling all the health food stores, as I had learned from my holistic studies that raw milk far surpassed pasteurized milk in its nutritional value and, in addition, had far fewer of the digestive and allergy problems associated with milk drinking. But at least I got the doctor's approval for goat's milk.

The NG tube supplied Aaron the formula for the evening, and in the morning, Jerry went out to buy goat's milk. While he was gone, I sat with Aaron, so tempted to lift my shirt and let him get a few sips of my warm milk. Each time he rooted for my breast, it got harder and harder to resist. Almost predictably, I succumbed when I could resist no longer. It felt so good. But concerned with what the doctor said about monitoring feedings, I kept it brief.

Jerry peeked his head through the curtain I had closed around us for privacy. Barely keeping a straight face, I whispered, "Jer, I nursed Aaron. He did so well."

Sighing disapprovingly, he said, "Lori. You know you're not supposed to do that. Why can't we just do what the doctors say. You heard Dr. Berenstein yesterday. No more chicken legs, he said. He got me scared."

"It was only for a minute, don't worry. I'm not going to go against the doctor's orders, but that doesn't mean I won't question them. Maybe Aaron was able to suck from me means he could also suck from a bottle.

Maybe he's already strong enough. And maybe he's even hungry enough. And on top of that, there's other ways to fatten up a baby than feeding him junk food. We can do it with quality nutrition."

On the topic of nutrition, Jerry always conceded if he didn't already agree; he suggested we tell the nurse so she could get in touch with the doctor. Next hurdle crossed, the doctor gave orders for supplemental bottle feedings of my milk, goat's milk, or formula, our choice entirely.

Since I did not have the sensory gratification of Aaron close to my breast, sucking away to his heart's content, my milk supply was not up to par, so we tried the goat's milk. Aaron begged off the bottle within two sips of tasting the stuff. It was obvious I would need to try the formula.

Maybe Aaron picked up my vibes; over the next few days, the only milk he would drink, with any consistency, was mine. We even tried mixing the formula with my sparse milk supply; the goat's milk with mine, and the goat's milk with formula. If my milk was in the greater proportion, he'd sometimes drink the combination.

Within two days, we were moved to a regular room; this time with an even more phenomenal view, which we thoroughly enjoyed. I set up my tape machine with meditation music and relaxed into the task of feeding Aaron. Much to my surprise, Aaron was gaining weight much faster than expected, an enormous ounce every two days, inconceivable for an infant who had been through what he'd been through. I kept up the regime of expressing my milk and cutting it with goat's milk or formula to stretch it further, and by the end of the week, my milk production was back up to snuff. It must have had something to do with the fact that I was finally relaxed, or so I was told.

Periodically, I gave Aaron the real stuff straight from the source, and soon a week and a half had passed, the pediatrician ordering the removal of the NG tube and exclusive use of the bottle. Success again. Aaron kept up his weight gain for three days; as a result, we were granted a trial run of straight breast milk, provided, of course, I could produce what was needed.

Every morning, as was the usual routine, a nurse came into our room, removed Aaron's diaper and weighed him — my breasts apparently providing what I hoped they would. Joyously, we received the news that we would be able to go home in a couple more days.

Chapter Fourteen

✳

It was late August, a full three weeks since Aaron had entered the hospital. Life was back to normal, Jerry working and me thoroughly enjoying being at home with my two boys. We were followed by the pediatric cardiologist twice a month for the first month and then once more at the end of October, by which time Aaron's heart had returned to its normal size, his height and weight falling well within the charts.

Sometime in late September, Jerry and I were attending a seminar for a nutritional product around which we had built a home-based business. As usual, Jeffrey enjoyed computer at his Grandma and Grandpa's, while we kept Aaron in tow. He was young enough to remain in a car seat most of the time.

Like most infants, Aaron attracted the usual attention from many of the seminar attendees. Jerry and I sat on the outside aisle with Aaron in his car seat right beside me. The morning session ended and we, along with one hundred other people, piled into the dining room for a buffet lunch. After serving ourselves,

Jerry and I sat down at a table, Aaron again next to me on the floor.

Sometime into the meal, I felt a hand tap my shoulder. I turned and noticed a strawberry blonde-haired woman in her early fifties standing between Aaron and me, someone I had never seen in the almost two years we had been attending these seminars. Her eyes looked straight through mine as she softly asked, "I don't want you to think I'm nosy, but what's wrong with your son's heart?"

I was flabbergasted. Her words pierced, forcing the air right out of me. I grabbed my chest and felt my heart racing. No, I thought, I must have heard her incorrectly.

I looked at her again, examining her face with my discerning eyes, certain I had never met her before. The chances of her knowing about Aaron were infinitesimally small. Tentatively, I replied, "What did you say?"

She repeated herself. "What's wrong with your son's heart?"

Now I knew I had heard her correctly the first time. I felt suspended, part of me cautiously anticipating assistance of some sort and part of me thinking this whole thing inconceivable. Seeking resolution, I looked closely at her again. Since I'd never met her before, and no one at this seminar knew anything of Aaron's ordeal, how did she know this piece of my three-dimensional world?

How could she know, I asked myself? Was she psychic?

Over the past eight years of consciously pursuing a spiritual path in life, I'd had numerous soulful and life-changing sessions with psychics and channelers, enough so I certainly knew how to distinguish the legitimate from the phony. The suspension I felt ceased. As if my sixth sense were activated, I knew this woman was here to help. Thirsting to know more, I asked, "How do you know?"

"I just know," she said with soft confidence, "I just know. May I work on him a little?"

Although this woman was essentially evading my questions, I knew what she guarded close to heart, what she wouldn't let on in words for fear I'd think her crazy.

I knew, without a shadow of a doubt, this woman was a healer. What kind of healer was not important. That she wanted to help Aaron was. I knew our serendipitous meeting had to have been divinely guided, so the same must be so for her "work."

My knowing was the profound kind, it resonated in my solar plexus, subtle yet absolute. From the moment she asked if she could work on Aaron, my inclinations were confirmed. There were no visual or auditory revelations, no Holy Spirit coursing through my body, not even a sweaty palm. I just knew. Simply knew. And I knew not to question that inner knowing, that God-given gift I'd out of ignorance questioned and not followed too often in the past. My insides rested in harmony with my thoughts; there was no internal tug of war for a change. Just a feeling of peace and of wholeness. I went with it.

"Sure," I responded, gratitude abounding. I felt like I'd just been given the grandest gift in the world. I intuitively trusted this woman with the blessed creation from mine and Jerry's lives, our innocent baby... this woman whom I'd never met, but knew intimately.

And so Edie and I, introduced and feeling safe, went back to the vacated conference room before the afternoon session while Jerry chatted with a few people. We sat Indian-style on the floor, leaning against the back wall as I told her more exactly of Aaron's condition, Edie listening quietly, making certain haunting comments as if she already knew.

Aaron was cradled in my arms, his head almost in Edie's lap. She held her hands slightly over his head and after a few tranquil minutes, remarked how the pulsating in the fontanelle was quieting down. She was right, it was definitely less marked. I remembered Dr. Berenstein explaining this pulse was that of the golf-ball sized fistula throbbing up against my son's delicate brain tissue. Could it be that in such a short time there was already a decrease in blood flow to that area?

Of that I wasn't sure, but the mechanics of what Edie was doing were not alien to me. I had, before marriage and children, studied therapeutic massage and taken workshops to learn to work with healing energy. I brought this work to my profession, often holding my hands over patients' pained body parts and frequently getting positive results. I could even feel the energy moving down my arms and out the palms of my hands. I felt privileged to be able to help my patients in this manner, and always wished I could be a vessel for permanent healing. But I was a novice. Edie, I sensed, had far more experience.

Edie continued to hold her hands over Aaron's head. I felt as though I was in a far-away place, in a clouded dream, removed from the reality of my life. My heart was wide open, totally receptive to Edie's selfless love.

I remained quite stunned yet cognizant of my gratitude for this co-incidence. But a coincidence it was not, at least as commonly defined. Contemplating my life in hindsight, I'd come to appreciate the perfect order of circumstances designing it. Any one piece missing, added, or placed differently would have ushered forth quite a different me. In fact, sometimes that which I cursed ended up being precisely what I needed to capture my visions.

I believe that coincidences happen all the time and that generally, we are not tuned in enough to realize they are happening. We almost need a mind-set that not only allows, but encourages coincidences in our lives. Inherent in that mind-set is the energy required to see them happening each and every day. Experience has taught me to believe nothing in life is by accident. I am convinced that every minutia of every event is interconnected, coinciding if you will. We only need to open our minds to that possibility, and it will begin to manifest, solidifying the belief that coincidence is simply and grandly the purposeful dance of divine order.

And that's how I saw Edie's entrance into my life. I accepted it as a totally natural occurrence, divine order orchestrating that which I favored first over the medical route. I certainly never would have denied my child necessary intervention. I am not that brazen; however, when there is breathing room, my practice is to first put to use any number of non-invasive approaches.

Before the end of the day, I felt like I had connected with a soul-mate. A most loving and giving soul-mate. I felt totally connected to Edie; her heart was one I recognized as my own. Profoundly moved by her entrance into our lives, I embraced her as if we'd come home to one another.

Jerry was formally introduced and, I'd say, open to my experience, but not deeply believing, as I was, that Edie's healing energy would help. Before we left for the day, Edie gave me her address and phone number, offering to do a group healing for Aaron with some of her close friends the following week.

How could I say no? Healing work sat much better with me than surgical intervention. It didn't matter to me that Edie would have other people participating. My trust in her at this point unwavering, I hoped this would keep us from another visit to New York University's Pediatric Unit. Anything to avoid surgical intervention enticed me.

Edie had her own version of what happened this historic day, a story she guarded for over a year. It was my relating the following incident to her that urged the story forth:

Not typical of my work as an occupational therapist, I found myself inclined to counsel an elderly Hispanic patient, as she was having a very difficult time relating with her quite proficient home health aide. I was talking to her for a good five minutes, attempting to have her see the aide's admirable intentions and trust her professional judgment, but to no avail. My patient was interrupting me frequently in her own self-defense, and in my opinion, was in need of a drastic alteration of perception, as she was finding fault where no fault was founded. Rather suddenly, I noticed my patient no longer interrupting me, but rather focusing quite intently on my words. Simultaneously, I noticed my words flowing forth, with little conscious thought on my delivery. The words continued for another ten minutes and when the words ceased, my patient looked at me and quite earnestly said, "There was an elderly Jewish man with a long black coat and hat, long hair, a real religious man, standing beside you the whole time you were talking. He was turning pages in a book, as though it was him speaking through you. When you were done, he closed the book and walked away."

One by one, each hair on my skin quivered, the chilling sensation verifying to me the authenticity of her statement. This was an extraordinary confirmation, absolute proof of my spirit guide. While not surprised, I was still stunned by the vivid description. I can't remember exactly when this entity came into my awareness, and in fact, I don't have any ongoing communication with him — at least any I'm aware of. But I had been told about this guide numerous times in the past by clairvoyants I sought for spiritual council. This, however, was unsolicited, confirmation of the best kind. Contemplating my connection to all things in God's universe, I smiled gratefully for yet another sign.

I drove home later in the day, still mesmerized and excited to tell Edie, my dear friend and spiritual compatriot. We'd come to be the warmest and most honest of friends, sharing our most intimate thoughts about life, love, our men, and the very essence of our womanhood. She was there for me in my times of need, times when our journey with Aaron became troubled. Edie's values regarding spiritual matters, a carbon copy of my own, enabled her to supportively remind me of my beliefs, my faith, and my own inner strength. Much more than a friend, she was like a wise spiritual sister guiding me when I needed, and like the best of mentors, challenging me to expand into greater spiritual awareness the moment I was ready.

I dialed Edie's number as soon as I arrived home. Thank God, the real person instead of the usual tape machine. I passionately shared my experience with her.

"You have some time, Lori?" she asked.

"Sure. Why?" I asked.

"Well, now that you're telling me this, I'll tell you the whole story of how I knew Aaron needed help. At the time, I didn't think you were ready to hear it," she said. "But now, I know you are."

Edie launched into her story. "The day that I met you, I was sitting in the back of the conference room feeling a very strong connection with Aaron. He kept arching back and looking over the top of the chair.

"Then, out of nowhere, this elderly Chasidic man, that your patient described, appeared alongside you and Aaron.

"He said to me, 'Come here, please. I need your help.'

"As if there were somebody else he was talking to, I said, 'You're talking to me?' If anyone saw me talking into the air, they would have thought me crazy. Then the spirit said, 'Yes, you. My little Chanala needs your help. Please. Come. Help my little Chanala.'

"I asked the spirit, 'Who's Chanala?'

"He answered, 'The baby. Help him. Please.'

"Meanwhile, I had no idea what was wrong with Aaron, so I asked him and he told me to ask you. Of course I told him I never met you and that you'd probably think me crazy, but he insisted. Then he just vaporized."

"What did you think, Edie?" I asked, knowing I would have been a little shaken, to say the least.

"What was I supposed to think?" she responded. "Anyway, who's Chanala?"

"Chanala is my grandmother's Hebrew name. Aaron was named after her."

Emphatically, Edie went on, "Well that's not all that happened, Lori. Then Aaron started looking back at me again. He was telepathically begging me to talk to you, saying he needed my help. He said something was wrong with his heart and that you could tell me more about it. But I wasn't ready to go over and talk to you yet."

Edie took a deep breath. "Then my guides started in on me. They said, 'This is the baby, this is the one. We told you about him. He helped you in a past life. Now, it's your turn to help him.'

"I hadn't done any healing work for almost three years because I was still recuperating from an antimalaria drug I was given when I was in India. I was sick as a dog from this drug and the last thing I wanted was to get back into my work. But my guides kept telling me to go over to you. And that's how I ended up asking you what was wrong with Aaron's heart."

From Edie's story, I gathered the airwaves were very busy that day in the seminar room. More fervently than ever, I believed they were always busy, busy helping orchestrate the events of our often unsettling lives. Again, I was reminded to hold steady my peace of mind and to trust in the perfection of all that had happened thus far and everything yet to unfold. All was in perfect order, in balance, and as I long suspected, the spirit world full of messengers and angels propelling us along our paths. The fact that I, throughout Aaron's ordeal, was continually being shown something to celebrate, amazes me, leaving me to this day feeling especially graced.

Chapter Fifteen
✳

With great expectation, I looked forward to the day I would bring Aaron to Edie's home. On the other hand, Jerry's feelings were neither positive nor negative. Over the years, Jerry has cultivated the ability to consistently give me latitude when needed, and then support me in my endeavors to boot. A rare quality, I know, and one for which I give thanks. And so, he felt if taking Aaron to Edie enhanced my peace of mind, he would not stand in my way. Yet, there was also a part of him that hoped this "healing stuff," as he put it, would help.

As I stepped out of the shower the morning of this patiently awaited day, his ambivalence surfaced a bit more. "How do you know she's legitimate?" he asked, poising a controversial question just when I needed to focus my thoughts on hustling my body out the door.

Feeling impatient, I unintentionally responded in an abrupt manner, "I don't know. I have no way of scientifically proving it." Catching myself offending his vulnerability, I reminded myself that although our belief systems were fundamentally similar, the previous seven years I had dedicated to soul searching and focused study strengthened my foundation and advanced my intuitive skills.

I softened both my tone and non-verbal expression, reassuringly placing my hand on his arm. "Listen, Sweets, I feel, deeply feel it's the right thing to do. I believe very strongly that this would not have landed in our path to not be taken advantage of. And besides, how would she have known what was wrong with Aaron in the first place?"

As usual, Jerry responded to my sensitivity far better than my abruptness. He acquiesced. "You've got a point. I hope it makes a difference," he said, almost pleadingly. Still with towel wrapped around me, I went into the embrace of his arms.

Getting through these impasses was not always so easy. Callous expression and anger frequented the early years of our marriage, Jerry and I each coming to the relationship with an entire baggage car full of painful experiences from childhood and past relationships. Thank God for love. That and a combination of our commitment and continual work on self enabled us to heal some of our buried pains, thus relating to each other with more open, loving hearts. It's an ongoing process in which we're involved, one which takes a certain brand of tenacity, and one to which we have become more committed through time. I said, "I love you," and kissed him, assuring him everything would be all right.

As most babies on long rides, Aaron was fast asleep by the time I arrived in Manhattan. I parked directly across the street from Edie's Upper West Side apartment, and to avoid waking Aaron, carried him up the two flights of stairs in his car seat.

Edie embraced me the moment I walked in. I felt taken care of and safe in her arms. I was introduced to three people, her daughter, Lisa, and two very dear male friends, John and Chuck.

I walked around for a few minutes as Edie excused herself to ready a few last details. Her studio was obviously an expression of her taste, interests, education, and extensive travels.

Hardwood floor, Oriental rug, antique desk, beautiful quartz crystals, sculptures, and East Indian artifacts all brought warmth and beauty to the room. A Master's of Social Work degree was on her wall as was a license to practice psychotherapy. I wondered if she integrated her diverse spiritual values into her therapy sessions. Next, I noticed a picture of Sai Baba, a guru with an ashram in India, visited by untold thousands from every corner of the world. I had read two books about this complex holy man and felt a strong affinity to his spiritual teachings. I smiled to myself. Another connection made.

Within ten minutes of my arrival, Chuck took me aside to tell me about his infirm infant son and how Edie had helped him to wellness, despite medical odds. His son had nevi, congenital growths on the underside of his scalp which, in his case, were pushing their way through the skull and into the brain. Yet another confirmation of my being in the right place doing the right thing.

I was called over to the corner of the room and asked to bring a still-sleeping Aaron. Laid out on the floor was a most delicate white lace antique baby blanket, speaking to the purity and innocence of Aaron's being. It lent an air of sanctity to the labor of love at hand, an honor to his soul.

Encircling the perimeter of the blanket, we each took our places, Edie asking me to take Aaron from his car seat. I doubted he would stay sleeping through the maneuver and wondered how she would do healing work on him while he expressed his outrage at being awakened.

Making me right with regards to my thoughts, Aaron started crying the moment I picked him up. Uncomfortable, I brought him to my lap, thinking I would nurse him back to sleep. Edie, sounding like she knew what she was doing, said, "Put him on the blanket, face up."

Thoughts scurried through my mind. Face up. Ridiculous. She hasn't the vaguest idea what it's like putting this one to sleep. I pictured my nightly routine with Aaron, my sitting with enduring patience as he resisted the effects of my manna, eventually nursing himself to sleep, only to have him wake up the moment I placed him in his crib. Of two things I was certain: The odds of his falling back to sleep were next to nothing; the odds of his falling back to sleep on his back were flat-out nothing. Hesitating, I put him on the blanket just as she said, my discomfort intensifying in direct proportion to the tenor of his crying.

"John," she said. "Hold the soles of Aaron's feet." I focused in on this man who I didn't know, this man who was now holding Aaron's feet. He was a distinguished, almost mysterious looking, prematurely silver-haired man with a very trim beard and mustache. He and Edie had a way of working together, which caused me to half-suspect they were in a relationship.

Edie cradled Aaron's head with her hands, Aaron fussing for all of five seconds and then falling right back to sleep. I could barely believe my eyes.

Edie began. Three times she said, "I invoke the light of the Christ within." She continued with a special prayer for Aaron and asked the rest of us to hold our hands over his body, visualizing love and light. We sat in focused prayer, the healing energy working for about a half-hour. Before long, each one of us was coming out of our meditation-like experiences. Aaron awoke a happy, rested camper.

I stayed a while longer and mingled with Edie's friends, Edie playing a most gracious hostess. Before I left, she asked me to come to her home in Long Island. "I mentioned Aaron in a prayer group last week and two of the women in the group, Christian Charismatics, almost fell out of their chairs. They were guided, they said, to work on your son. Will you come with Aaron sometime the week after next?"

Let me think a second... yes! I felt like a kid in a candy shop being offered the opportunity to indulge in a whole pound of the best milk chocolate.

The next two weeks flew by.

I arrived at Edie's home in Long Island shortly before lunch. The first to arrive, I helped Edie with the finishing touches on her menu, a particularly Jewish spread of food much like that seen at a briss, the ceremonial circumcision of the eight-day-old Jewish boy. But then again, who was I to judge what to serve for a healing service?!

Before long, Edie's friends, Joanne, Carol, and Debbie, arrived, and after introductions, we sat down to lunch. My conservative Jewish background had me feeling like a foreigner in a strange land. With Christian Charismatics, I was clueless, not knowing what to expect. But I found these women entirely likable, sincerely interested in helping Aaron.

By the time lunch was cleaned up, I found myself anxious to begin. What would this Christian healing service look like, I wondered? Would it be different than other forms of healing I had previously been exposed to? Despite my metaphysical orientation and belief that the religions we were born to or practiced were of little import, my hypnotic Judaic indoctrination made it difficult to bridge the differences inherent in our two faiths. Freeing my mind from the biased teachings of over-zealous Jewish educators, bent on keeping innocent minds cloistered and merely tolerant of their Christian counterparts, was no easy feat.

We all sat on the carpet in Edie's living room. Joanne, having changed into an all-white, gauze-like cotton ceremonial outfit, looked almost angelic, enhancing the holy essence of our gathering. She sat Indian-style with Aaron cradled in her arms, he taking to her instantaneously. The intimacy established by these women caused my lingering anxiety to dissolve into nothingness.

In fact, all three of the women were taken by Aaron, something I had come to expect yet not take for granted. It was something in and of him, a quality, an air — it attracted loving people around him. It wasn't his cuteness. Of course he was cute... I'm his adoring mother. But this was something different. I believe it had to do with his spirit, his true nature — the nature inherent, yet somewhat blocked within most of us because of our painful early life experiences. It caused love to pour forth from anyone who came in contact with him; as though on an energetic level, he drew it out of them. Indeed, watching his effect on people was rather magical.

While Joanne held Aaron, the other two women quietly prayed. Candles burned around the ceremonial area, Christian ornaments enhancing the sanctity. An inward focus on God for a few moments, and then I followed the women and Edie as they faced their palms towards Aaron.

Within a few minutes, Joanne's body started to tremble slightly, the Holy Spirit, I suspected, running through her body and into Aaron's. I had been acquainted with this sensation a few times in my life. It feels like a staccato vibration conducting itself through the cellular structure of your body, each cell connecting to an adjacent cell until the energy has coursed entirely through, leaving behind a blissful delicate hum. I liken it to the phenomenon of electricity.

I watched Joanne's body quiver and thanked the consciousness that poured through her. All I had come to believe in my life, through my own spiritual searching, was being revealed to me. I'm not totally sure, but I'd venture a guess that Wayne Dyer wasn't the first to conceptualize the saying, you need to believe it before you see it, although I like his non-religion-specific way of saying it.

Within twenty minutes, Joanne's body had become still, and slowly, she opened her eyes. Her face was radiant. She had a benevolence about herself and I could tell something remarkable had happened for her too. I felt a union with these women, a spiritual "at home" feeling. God gave us life to do such great service for one another, I thought. I was tremendously grateful for the time, energy, and love they bestowed upon me and Aaron.

Obviously in an altered state, it took Joanne about five minutes to get grounded, to become fully engaged in the present. When she was, we graced the healing with closing prayers of thanks.

Before we departed, Edie and her friends agreed that another healing service, one at my house, was in order. We set a date for one month hence.

I can't say I noticed anything remarkable with Aaron over the next four weeks, but in looking forward to an MRI within the next couple of months, and a subsequent embolization, I was most agreeable to have any healing work, in fact, anything non-invasive done for Aaron.

Edie requested I prepare lunch as she had done a month earlier. Dutifully, I prepared autumn squash soup, bought a hearty loaf of whole grain bread, and made a huge bowl of salad. Lunch was a hit, the women asking for my soup recipe. I was a bit anxious as last time, but for none of the same reasons. This time it was because my parents would be paying me a visit sometime mid-afternoon. I had told them about Edie and the healing work being done on Aaron, mostly addressing the issue using semantics in and around the word prayer. Surprisingly, they didn't voice objections. Then again, I didn't say more than I had to so as not to confront their Jewish sensibilities. Perhaps I judged them harshly, but I figured it hard enough to swallow healing; I didn't need to add fuel to the fire and have them fear their only daughter, brought up to be a lifelong, card-carrying Jew, turning Christian.

We gathered on the rug in my family room, statues of Jesus and Mary, rosary beads, a wooden cross, a Bible, and candles all placed thoughtfully throughout the room. The experience was most gratifying, basically the same as the previous healing at Edie's house, but this time Joanne's body did not tremble. Again, I was grateful for the love and energy coming forth from these women.

We were just about done and I heard a knock at the door. Edie looked out the window. "Who has a gray Oldsmobile?" she asked.

I looked out the same window. "Oh, nuts. It's my parents! They're early!" I was frantic. It was only two-thirty. All the shades were drawn with the only lights coming from candles placed strategically around the room.

Like a hurricane sweeping across an open plain, we restored that room in under one minute. All the

Christian relics needed, due to my fear, to be out of sight from four highly judgmental Jewish eyes. Edie understood — she was raised in the same manner. I opened the front door, embraced my parents, and, heart pounding so fiercely I thought it audible, introduced them to Edie and her friends. To this day, I have no idea what my parents were thinking and never asked. Some things are better left untouched.

Chapter Sixteen

✳

Aaron, now four-months-old and clinically doing very well, was scheduled by Dr. Berenstein for a second procedure, one week before a conference at which this internationally recognized practitioner would present a paper on his highly specialized procedure. I assumed he wanted to make absolutely sure we were free and clear for him to travel to France, not requiring any further assistance.

In lieu of the procedure, an MRI was required for the beginning of January in order to define the extent of the work left to be done. We scheduled it at a nearby medical center, an experience I shall never forget.

Due to the fact one must lie perfectly still when in the MRI apparatus, Aaron needed to be sedated beforehand. Chloral hydrate was the drug of choice, the strawberry-flavored variety, a most delicious elixir. I had everything set to administer the first dosage in the car on the way to the medical center so Aaron would have a good half hour to surrender to its effects.

Jerry drove. I had Aaron in the front passenger seat

with me, poised to give him his drink via eyedropper, but my little tyke out-smarted me. He pulled away as I let the first few drops into his mouth. Realizing I'd have to deceive him somewhat, I lifted my shirt and had him nurse a few minutes, then stuck the dropper in the corner of his mouth and put him back on my breast to wash it down. It worked, but that was only the first half of the dosage. Who knew if he'd fall for the same trick a second time.

With Aaron almost under the spell, I inserted the dropper again, administered the rest of the dosage, and for auxiliary power, placed him back on my breast. He sucked happily for about two minutes and then dropped into a sweet slumber.

Everything went according to schedule, that is, until we arrived at the clinic. As I carefully got out of the car, Aaron awoke from a deep sleep, floppy, drowsy, and obviously under the influence. Unfortunately, he wasn't too interested in nursing anymore, so I couldn't push him over the edge in the preferred manner.

Once we entered the waiting area, we gave Aaron the back-up dosage, this only making Aaron that much more rubber-like. The technician waited patiently as I tried to nurse Aaron to sleep, but every attempt, once I stood up to walk over to the testing room, ended with Aaron's opening his eyes.

Four failed attempts and I decided to try a new tactic, so I took Aaron, still sucking, over to the platform on which he was to lay, and gently laid him down. Ever so smoothly, I removed my breast from his mouth and before I got to back away, he poked up his head and back on he latched, despite being totally wiped out from the chloral hydrate. Finally, thinking he had surrendered to sleep, I pulled away. But his homing instincts were still intact, despite his drugged state. Within seconds, he started arching and rooting for me as if it were my arms cradling him, not the padded platform.

I stood on some steps next to the platform more than ten minutes, attempting several times to leave Aaron sleeping restfully, Jerry, in the meantime, standing by to climb onto the apparatus so he could lie within arm's reach of Aaron once the platform was moved into place. The whole fiasco was really quite comical, the technician, I'm sure, getting ample laughs for the day.

Mission accomplished, the test began. I paced the hall for the twenty-minute duration, and through a shaded thick-paned glass, I studied the computer that displayed images of Aaron's brain. But this was a technology I had never been exposed to before. I could not decipher the pictures.

When the test was over, Jerry emerged with an awake but groggy Aaron, no worse for the wear and tear. We waited for a little while, hopeful of getting results, but unfortunately were told we'd have to get the results from Dr. Berenstein directly. No need to wait longer, the laboratory would send the MRI film to Dr. Berenstein.

We got a verbal report about three days later. Although we were told the rate of blood flow through the fistula appeared to have slowed down quite a bit, the vein of Galen was still abnormally dilated, so the next procedure was confirmed for Aaron twelve days later.

Maybe the healing work had helped to slow the blood flow. Maybe not. We wouldn't know anything for sure until Dr. Berenstein snaked his catheters through Aaron's veins a second time. With fervent desire, we counted down the days, somewhere between hoping and counting on this procedure being the last.

Chapter Seventeen

✳

Our second admission to NYU was a bit less stressful than the first; the routine questions and blood tests, quite familiar. Ironically, I was beginning to feel like an old pro in this institution whose methods of dealing with illness I chose not to align with except in the case of no alternatives. I would have liked to have avoided this, but the MRI showed Aaron's condition, while better, still required the skilled intervention of Dr. Berenstein's gifted hands.

Interestingly, I did not question the efficacy of the healing work either, or in any way judge it to have not achieved the desired results. I knew not what to expect from the spiritual intervention; I only knew that in general, it would support Aaron's life. And I trusted that it would only support Dr. Berenstein in his efforts.

In addition, I did not feel it my place to dictate the manner in which Aaron would move towards wellness. I felt no resentment or anger about the fact that Aaron required additional surgical intervention.

I just prayed and trusted — prayed a lot and trusted strongly that Dr. Berenstein, with the help of Edie and her Charismatic Christian friends, would do a second procedure, bringing an end to our struggles.

That's not to say I didn't fear for Aaron's life periodically. Quite the opposite. Like any mother, I can't stand the thought of my child suffering. When the fear crept in, and of course it was when I was most unsuspecting, I tried my best to chase it from my mind. "Cancel that thought," I'd say to myself. "Cancel, cancel, cancel." I'd visualize a big X over any image I had in my mind, shrink it, and move it further and further away until it was no longer visible. Sometimes the image would creep back and then I'd visualize even bolder X's, one over the next, over the next.

In the previous seven years, I had learned of the mind's power to manifest with thought. In other words, I learned how our minds dictate our experiences in the world, or more specifically, our perception of our experiences. I learned I needed to keep my mind positive, clear of negative thoughts, in order to alter the turn of events in my life back then, a time of great difficulty. I was going through a painful divorce, thankfully no children, but painful nonetheless. My life appeared to be changing daily. I was looking at supporting myself in the manner to which I had become accustomed; I was confused, angry, and feeling quite alone. A friend, recognizing the pain I was suffering, recommended I see his psychic. I had never been to a psychic before, let alone think about these matters. I wasn't closed to the idea, but I wasn't open either. Nor was I a skeptic. My mind was a clear slate for I had no previous programming, parental, social, or religious. In great need of a peaceful heart, I called the psychic and booked an appointment, giving only my name for information.

I arrived at the psychic's apartment a week later hoping to find answers to put my worries to rest. Carmella, the psychic, was a woman in her early sixties, a grandma-type. Her home was filled with a horde of elephant statues, each trunk symbolically pointing towards the door to chase away evil. She lit a candle which sat on the dining room table next to Mother Mary. Quietly she prayed, and then started to talk to me.

Carmella had no way of knowing anything about me, and yet she knew everything about me. She knew of my divorce, my fear of supporting myself, and many things I no longer remember. At one point, I was reduced to tears, for she had exactly described the emotional tenor of my very existence. She revealed to me the essence of what I fought hard to hide, thus releasing me from my own inner constriction. I was beholden.

Before leaving that afternoon, Carmella recommended I read a book called "Three Magic Words," by U.S. Anderson. That book changed my life. It spoke of metaphysical truths and the ability to change the circumstances in one's life by carefully monitoring and then changing the negative thoughts in one's head. It offered a positive mental diet whereby, for thirty days, I was to think only positive about any of the circumstances that came my way. If something negative happened, I was to say, "I will see the light in this," over and over, replacing the darkness with light.

I started this mental diet and blew the whole program at least three times, starting over each time until I eventually sailed through and beyond the thirty-day period. One day while working, I was driving to my next patient down a street in the south Bronx, at a time well before its renovation. I stopped my car, taken by the sight of three quite young and beautiful Hispanic kids playing in the burnt-down rubble of an ancient apartment building. I gazed at them, totally drawn to their innocence. A few minutes later, I proceeded on down the street and within fifty yards; I brought my car to a screeching halt. "Holy ----!" I said out loud, the words involuntarily flying out my mouth. "I saw the kids and not the burnt-down rubble."

At that precise moment, I realized what I had accomplished with my mind. I thought about my life, my current circumstances, and the promise of the whole program I had religiously stuck to and accomplished. Many things had changed. Some hadn't. But these things no longer sent me flying into the fits of anger or depths of sadness I had experienced just thirty some-odd days prior. I got it. From this experience, I knew I had the power to change the events in my life by guarding the thoughts I held in my head — a lesson I've never forgotten, a practice I perpetually attempt to perfect, my situation with Aaron included.

And so I vacillated between X-ing out fear and total faith in Aaron's healing. I kept telling myself not to question the journey, but rather to hold the goal clearly in mind. Some days were easier than others, but all in all, I believe I triumphed.

Since I believe that all things happen for reasons and that something can be learned from each life incident, I also had half a suspicion that Aaron was to require medical intervention, in part so I would learn to soften my rigid values regarding the allopathic community and honestly acknowledge their value as well. Truly, I would have preferred my road to have been that of a Christian Scientist, with, of course, a guarantee clause — for Aaron's sake, and in all honesty, for my ego as well. I loved to prove a point when it came to my beliefs. But it was not the right time to prove a point. Rather, what felt right was to surrender to what was, or what in Yiddish is called besherdt, meant to be.

Edie and her friend John came to visit us in the early evening, gracing us with a delicious meal of Chinese food. Aaron, tired from the day's events, had fallen asleep in my arms, and Edie, full of wanting to be a grandma herself, took him from my arms and placed him in his crib. Funny, but I found it impossible to make that transition without his awaking, Aaron accurately sensing my first thought of putting him in his crib!

We talked, we prayed, and we thanked God that evening, Edie reinforcing in my mind that God works not only through the healer's hands, but the physician's hands as well.

Aaron went off to the surgery room at seven the following morning. More familiar with the ropes and the tendency towards mental anguish, I chose to wait through the day visualizing my little Aaron being delivered to me in the early afternoon, able to say good-bye to the hospital scene for good. Jerry, at my side, had my attitude this time. So we waited. We were waiting like we had placed an order for some food... sure to receive exactly what we expected.

As I'm the more contemplative one of the two of us, I stayed put most of the day. Jerry, on the other hand, strolled around the corridors, playing with children and empathizing with parents.

He introduced me to a family he met; they had traveled all the way from Michigan to find help for their eighteen-month-old daughter, Amber. Precious little one, she had a malignant tumor spanning the distance between her midbrain and top few cervical vertebrae. The doctors from their neck of the woods said it was inoperable and that it would eventually take her life. Not willing to be content with that response, they sought the advice of numerous neurosurgeons and ended up at NYU with a Dr. Wisoff and his associates. The competent doctors surgically removed all that was possible, approximately three-quarters of this life-threatening growth. I thought us lucky to have our problems and our Dr. Berenstein. Never would I have traded places.

What was early in the afternoon got to be three, then four, and finally at four-thirty, Dr. Berenstein met us in the parents' room. I held my breath as he sat down on the couch adjacent to us, the look on his face a full octave down from happy.

"Don't worry," he said. "Aaron's okay. We found only two arteries left to close when we went in, but I wasn't able to close them down." Jerry and I groped for each other's hands as he went on.

"With your permission, I'd like to try again tomorrow. Access up the right leg. Today we tried snaking the catheters up the left side of the body. I'm thinking we might get a different angle from the right side."

Jerry and I just sat there, stunned. This was the last thing either of us expected.

Dr. Berenstein took a pen from his lab coat and went to write on a napkin lying on the coffee table. He drew a vessel running straight from south to north. Midway, shooting off the right side of this vessel, he drew a narrower vessel, and then continued its path as it proceeded northeast slightly, and directed it through a hair-pin turn heading due south. He pointed his pen at the south-to-north vessel, frustration oozing out the lines in his forehead.

"Many times and from various vantage points, we tried to head up this artery and unfortunately, we couldn't advance the catheter past the point where the smaller vessel shoots off." He pointed his pen at the vessel making the hair-pin turn. "Every time I went in, I kept getting stuck in this artery. But I needed to go further up the other artery and close that one first."

I thought I got what he said, but had no idea why it had to be in that order. The state of shock subsided only minimally, acting as an analgesic to my own propensity to require concrete reasons for everything. Later on, I figured out that if he closed the smaller vessel first, he risked having the larger vessel, already stretched near capacity, burst, unable to accommodate any greater volume of blood flow.

Impatiently awaiting the final word, the precise details of his next tactic, I asked with a trembling voice, "So you want to try again tomorrow?" The thought of waiting with bated breath another day was anything but appealing.

"Aaron will be coming back to the ICU any minute. I left the catheters from this morning in place and splinted his legs to prevent them from being pulled out. Leaving the catheters intact will save us an hour and a half with the anesthesia tomorrow. I'm hoping if I access the malformation from the right side, I'll have better luck."

What was there to say? In our minds, there were no options.

Dr. Berenstein instructed us that Aaron would be very mildly sedated to keep him still. There was to be no feeding, breast or otherwise.

"No feeding?" I complained to Jerry, after Dr. Berenstein had left. "How am I even going to get near Aaron without him wanting to nurse?"

And so the all-night vigil between father and son began. I saw Aaron briefly in the ICU. He was drowsy, just as Dr. Berenstein had said. His legs were splayed apart, rotated outward. Catheters were taped over the place they entered the groin and his legs were taped to primitive-looking flat wooden splints. His hands were also loosely restrained to support the effort of keeping the catheters intact. It looked horribly restricting, and I cringed, wondering what Aaron was aware of, if he felt pain, and oh God, if he'd be able to go the night without me. How close we had become through this ordeal. But God must have had in mind something else, perhaps a time for early father and son bonding!

I went to sleep in the parents' room that evening after kissing my sleeping Aaron and cajoling Jerry about not nodding out, as they didn't allow parents to sleep in the ICU. Inside, I was pained, stripped of my maternal responsibilities, and yet grateful for the much-needed full night's sleep I was to enjoy.

My steady husband stayed awake most of the evening; any time Aaron stirred, he was peering right over the top of the crib, assuring our son he was not alone. It was a time of some very soulful connecting with Aaron, a time for which Jerry is grateful. And this was a man who at that time unconsciously yearned to have his heart pried open a bit. Typically, mothers have the monopoly on early bonding. I'd agree with Jerry; he was lucky to have this time with Aaron. Oh, the gratification and peace of seeing the light in all God's workings.

Waking with the sun the next morning, Jerry and I watched Aaron go into the surgery room, this day carrying with it a heaviness that yesterday hadn't, the X-ing out not working as effectively. Yesterday's insult to my peace of mind had taken a larger toll than I would have liked.

I went up to the parents' room to get something from my suitcase while Jerry went to mingle with one of the other parents. From inside the closet, I heard the pay phone ringing.

"Hello, this is the parents' waiting room. May I help you?" I said.

"Lori, is that you? It's Edie."

"Hi. How are you?" I said, certainly not sounding my usual self. But it was as if Edie didn't hear me at all.

"Sit down, Lori. I have something important to tell you."

"What, Edie? Why?"

"Sit down." Sensing the importance in her voice, I did.

"Okay. I'm sitting," I told her.

"Lori, my guides were talking to me last night. You've got to tell this to Dr. Berenstein. Immediately."

"Your guides were talking to you last night?" I asked dubiously. I needed to make sure I heard her right. If she did have spirit friends from "the other side" who communicated with her, she never mentioned it to me. Not that what she was saying was ludicrous to me. I believe people have spirit guides assisting us on our life paths; I personally knew some people who channeled their guide's highest insights. But Edie never mentioned herself as being one of these types of psychics or healers, and for that reason, I needed a reality check.

"Yes, my guides were talking to me. They told me: There's a mighty river and a smaller river. The doctor's got to stay in the mighty river. The guides told me Aaron would be all right, that there are simple answers to simple questions. It's just that doctors look to do things the hard way, sometimes."

Now mind you, Jerry and I kept the news from the day before absolutely private. Edie knew nothing of Dr. Berenstein's findings, nor could she have known that at this moment, he was working on Aaron exactly as she described. Only a transfer of information as she described could have made her privy.

I looked up, as if to see God spread across the ceiling, the deepest knowing within my heart resounding in its complete and utter joy. There really is a higher power orchestrating what goes on down here, I thought. I felt so completely loved, my innermost needs so perfectly nurtured.

As tears of joy cascaded down my face, the empty space in the room turned a glowing opalescent misty white, which in a few moments began a swirling dance through and around me. Words cannot even begin to describe the intensity of emotion which filled me. I remember thinking it off-beat, Aaron being downstairs under anesthesia, and me being several floors above him, blissed out, in God's love and my very intimate experience with that love.

Recoiling from yet another almost expected shock, once again, Edie simply "knew." I sputtered words informing her of the accuracy in her guides' channeled information and of Aaron's present whereabouts. As with much of the metaphysical realm I had experienced, this one reigned supreme.

The vision, filling me for a lifetime, lasted but a few minutes. Between tears, I somehow reported to Edie the gift being bestowed upon me, she expressing her love for me in turn. I was unfolding spiritually and she was witness. No more perfect gift can the student give the teacher.

To this day, that experience has never left me and

when shared, always leaves people confirming their own faith, however little, which is just waiting to be tapped and sparked into light. It's especially nice when God's messages are clearly audible.

Quite high from the morning's experience, I waited optimistically for the afternoon's results. Jerry, not as moved by my spiritual experience, remained nervous. I wished my peace of mind on him.

Dr. Berenstein came to report to us around three in the afternoon. "I'm sorry," he said. I wasn't able to do it. Aaron's resting right now." This highly performance-oriented man was angry at himself and frustrated for stopping short of his goal.

My heightened feeling left rather suddenly. I was reduced from a blissed-out ecstasy to a fearful somberness, all in the space of a few minutes.

"I brought in Dr. Wisoff, the neurosurgeon, for a consultation during the procedure. He feels he can get the arteries surgically." His intensity deepened, as did the void in my chest. "Aaron also has some hydrocephalus and is going to need a shunt. You shouldn't have waited so long to have this second procedure done." This was the first I'd heard of this. It almost sounded like blame, but I knew, even in my heightened disappointment, it was his defensiveness, his frustration for not saving Aaron from the neurosurgeon's carving knife. "I'm sorry, but I'm going to have to place Aaron in his care," he said.

Jerry whispered, "Dr. Wisoff is the neurosurgeon who worked on Amber."

Even though he successfully removed three-quarters

of Amber's tumor, I was all but at ease.

My heart plummeted through my stomach. N-e-u-r-o-s-u-r-g-e-r-y. The big N. And a shunt too. My therapy background afforded me the opportunity to know these medical terms. Hydrocephalus means water on the brain. Somehow the water chambers that cushion the brain, the ventricles, were backing up with fluid and causing increased brain pressure. I imagined electric saws cutting away at Aaron's skull. Blood, parts of the brain moved aside, probes meandering through cavernous spaces to display the fistula and its feeding vessels. I looked up from my private thoughts and noticed that Dr. Berenstein had gone. I wasn't sure, but I thought I heard him say good-bye.

Pained, Jerry and I walked out into the hallway and leaned on the wall. All strength, mental and physical, was drained in the space of just a few minutes. Jerry turned to the wall, a wave of uncontrollable sobbing overtaking him. Never in the five and a half years we had been married had I seen him lose it like this. Nothing ever cut so deeply into the core of his being. The greatest gloom had befallen, my defensive X-ing out surrendering in desperate defeat. I now assessed us victims to an abhorrent scavenging system.

A rather clean-cut, dark-haired man in his mid-thirties was waiting for us, like a vulture waiting to feed off fresh carrion. He was dressed in a dark suit, looking sharp and shaven. Perhaps unfair, our impression, stemming from our naked vulnerability, pegged him quite the opposite of Dr. Berenstein, the casual, caring humanitarian.

"I'm Dr. Wisoff. I'll be Aaron's neurosurgeon." He shook both of our hands. I was in a daze, unable to process much of what the man in the dark suit was saying. He went on and on, the inappropriateness of this conversation following the onslaught of defeat, apparently not obvious to him, his bedside manner indiscreetly cast off-shore. There was something very opportunistic about his presentation, hence, up went our guard.

In an emotionless, calculating tone he explained how he could clip the artery surgically by cutting out a piece of the skull, going in between the left and right hemispheres of the brain, driving right through the corpus callosum. Red lights flashed in my brain... I was aware of them, even through my daze. The corpus callosum is the communicating fibers between the two hemispheres of the brain. Danger, I thought. Brain damage, a huge possibility. This was a turn for the worse.

Only aggravating matters more, the lack of warmth in this highly trained surgeon's, or should I say, intruder's voice had me considering alternatives. Here we'd just come from the fire and passion of our Latin compatriot. The iciness of Dr. Wisoff's presentation — talking about my child as though it was a basic shop class, left me feeling violated.

I was disappointed in God. After my God-given unbelievable spiritual experience this morning, I honestly had thought today would be the last. Experiences like mine, revelations, were absolute validations. I believed in the promise of Edie's channeling, believed the words to be certain, as if they were sourced by God himself. What was going on? Why the turn of events? I felt abandoned.

Dr. Wisoff invited us to his office to demonstrate on his brain models just exactly what he was going to do. I could tell he was responding to the look of shock on my face, my devastation over the day's outcome. But nothing he could say would put my mind at ease. My brain was rejecting the idea of neurosurgery, much like a computer rejects programs requiring too many megabytes. Over and over, my mind flipped through events as if somewhere I would find a flaw and arrive at a different conclusion, one better than God's.

"Come down to my office in about forty-five minutes. I just have a few things to attend to first," Dr. Wisoff said, as he walked towards the elevators. Gut-wrenched, the last thing I wanted was a detailed dissertation on what was to be my son's brain dissection. Obviously, our lives were still meant to be wrapped up in the throes of one of New York City's major medical centers.

Chapter Eighteen

✳

His office had diplomas displayed proudly on tired surgical-green walls and a desk made of expensive mahogany with several brain models standing by for the upcoming demonstration. Jerry and I waited while he finished a phone call. The Battle of the Bulge was about to begin.

"Here's a brain model on which I can show you exactly what I plan to do," he said. "First, we're going to have to saw out a section of Aaron's skull."

Horrified, we sunk in our chairs. "How do you saw it?" I had to ask.

"A typical electric saw."

My mind scanned its memory banks. Revealed to me like flashcards, the saws from my father's workshop when I was a kid displayed their awesome ability. All types of different edges, some jagged, some fine; which one was chosen depended on the material being cut. In this case it was Aaron's skull, and since his head was quite tiny, I visualized a four-inch blade, an electric saw with a very fine, razor-like edge, one that would make a clean cut. But first a razor to shave much of his beautiful blonde locks of hair, a patch one-quarter the size of his head. Next, the scalpel, cutting away a section of scalp under which the white glistening bone of his skull would be revealed. The saw turned itself on, its blade now rapidly gyrating. Its screeching reached notes at least two octaves higher as it eased into the bone. Careful, easy...don't nip the brain and there won't be any blood. I cringed at my mind's pictures. One cut made, the saw screeched its soprano notes again as it started the next cut right-angled to the first. It slipped and nicked a soft undulating fold in the brain, blood squirting all over. My devastation was complete. What hope did we have?

I returned to the present as Dr. Wisoff split open the hemispheres of the brain, showing how he would move through their connecting fibers, the corpus callosum. Then, he opened the hemispheres further, pointing to the third and fourth ventricles of the brain, the fluid housing centers. Thankfully, the models were free of blood.

"The fistula rests right here, right at the Aqueduct of Sylvius, the aqueduct between the third and fourth ventricles. Once we open this up, we'll see exactly how the malformed arteries lay and then clip them closed with surgical staples."

"What are the chances of brain damage?" Jerry asked.

"They're present. But it's a risk we have to take. I'm confident we'll be able to do our job in there, but there's a real chance there could be residual deficits."

Aaron might not need this surgery, I hoped. Aaron's telepathic communication to me about being all right had me picture healthy and normally developed. My mind would certainly have to grapple with this one.

"You know Aaron has also developed some hydrocephalus," he started.

We nodded. I had already explained what it was to Jerry.

"The standard treatment is to place a shunt in the brain to maintain normal pressure," he matter-of-factly said as he moved his brain model towards us. "What we will do is enter the brain to the left of the fontanelle, placing one end of the shunt right into the third ventricle of the brain. Then, we'll snake the other end of the shunt underneath the skin, following a path behind the ear, down the side of the neck, and down towards the abdomen where it will exit into the peritoneum, or abdominal cavity. In the peritoneum, there are plenty of blood vessels to absorb the fluid from the shunt, thereby recirculating it."

My mind vehemently rejected the concept. Something unnatural in the body. Not for one of my kids. I was on the attack.

"What is this shunt material made of?" I questioned.

"It's surgical tubing. Plastic," he answered.

"My son's not going to need the shunt forever," I said, optimistically.

"Once a shunt, always a shunt. I'm sorry to say, but it's true," he said.

"But you don't understand," I said. "This is my son."

He obviously didn't understand who he was dealing with. My brand of tenacity is rare.

"Once a shunt, always a shunt."

"But why?" I questioned, challenging his umpteen degrees and commendations.

"Once a shunt, always a shunt," he said once more.

Not a good enough answer, I thought. He's going to have to come up with something more substantial than that. "Once you close the malformed arteries in Aaron's brain, thereby alleviating the cause of the hydrocephalus, why then would you still require the shunt? It just doesn't make sense."

"Mrs. Gershon, never once in all my years have I ever had to remove a shunt because it was no longer needed," he insisted.

Given his tone, I was beginning to feel as if I might have been intruding on his professionalism. I felt I needed to explain myself. "Dr. Wisoff, you'll have to excuse me, but I'm an occupational therapist. I'm more familiar than most parents about what we're talking. Plus that, I have an extremely holistic approach towards health. Won't he have an immunological response to the plastic? I mean, it's not natural tissue you're putting in his body."

"No, Mrs. Gershon. That's never happened. You don't need to be concerned about that," he said. I could tell I was wearing his patience a little thin. Jerry reached over and touched my knee, reminding me to be polite, I suspected.

"But can't the plastic break down in his body? I mean, after all, doesn't all plastic break down after time?" I had mental pictures of a plastic water bottle breaking down and emitting toxins into the water it housed. That's why we used only glass. I knew the body wouldn't tolerate such goings-on in its interior.

"The shunt is made of an inert plastic," he explained. There is absolutely no chance of that happening.

"I still don't get it. I'm sorry. But if you go in and close off the malformed arteries, thereby alleviating the cause of the fistula and the hydrocephalus, why won't that mean he won't need the shunt? I know I'm repeating myself, but that one piece doesn't make sense."

"Mrs. Gershon, sometimes shunts malfunction and we have to put in new ones. And rarely, only rarely, have I ever come upon a shunt that is not working and where simultaneously, we discover there is no longer a need. Don't count on it, though, Mrs. Gershon."

"Thank you for the information," I sang out victoriously. I got what I wanted. A hole in his argument. Rarely, they find a not-working and not-needed shunt. For me, that was enough evidence on which to build my hopes of a shunt-free child. I was beginning to recover from the onslaught.

"Before you leave my office, I'll have my receptionist set an appointment for the surgery." Dr. Wisoff pushed his brain model aside, and went on to tell us about shunt maintenance and accidental malfunction. Projectile vomiting or high temperatures were signs of malfunction. I was counting on never needing to recall this information. After all, Aaron was not going to need the shunt forever.

Chapter Nineteen

✳

There was very little light in our lives the first few days we were home, nothing to laugh at and nothing about our quandary I could find to celebrate. Our days were filled with the purposeful activities of parenthood and household, what was to come weighing heavily in every saturated diaper, lingering with each spoonful of pureed food. The many phone calls with concerned friends or relatives only sank me deeper into my depressed state.

Neurosurgery is a word I could have lived without having in my vocabulary, let alone in my mind on a daily basis. All it conjured up were memories of patients, handicapped children and adults from craniotomies, secondary to very involved strokes or tumors. That's not to say the craniotomies were not successful. They were — in that they saved people's lives. But this was not a quality of life I could gracefully accept for my son.

I thought of the eighteen-month-old girl whose parents Jerry befriended. That was some incredibly delicate work Dr. Wisoff accomplished. I wondered which was more difficult and potentially more life-threatening: removing a tumor between the base of the brain and the spine or delving into actual brain tissue in hopes to isolate and seal off a particular formation of blood vessels. Any disturbance to the brain or the spinal column had the potential to enormously insult the integrity of the nervous system and cause great physical disability.

The days continued, little by little Jerry and I each accepting what would ensue in another three weeks. The energy of the devastation somehow re-formed itself. Hope reappeared and although suspended by the most delicate thread, it had the power to ease our pain. In devastation, there was no hope, no prayer, solely a victim's stance in relation to God. With acceptance, somehow, there was now room for a loving God. Albeit only slightly, the light was illuminating our existence again.

The day of our scheduled admission came. As instructed, we waited at home for the phone call which would let us know when a bed was free for Aaron. By three in the afternoon, we had not heard a word, my resistance to the neurosurgery having me quite passive in this matter. By four, though, I thought it wise to call the hospital.

It took five rings for someone to finally answer the phone. "Hello, Dr. Wisoff's office."

"Hi, this is Lori Gershon. My son Aaron is scheduled for surgery tomorrow with Dr. Wisoff, but as of yet, we've not gotten a call to come in and register."

"Hold on one minute," I was told.

I waited somewhat impatiently, thinking this whole thing quite ludicrous and unprofessionally handled. The receptionist got back on the phone.

"Mrs. Gershon, I just spoke with Dr. Wisoff's nurse and she informed me your son's surgery was rescheduled as Dr. Wisoff has had to take an emergency case tomorrow."

A huge sigh of relief. I fell into one of the kitchen chairs. "When are we rescheduled to?" I asked.

"A week from tomorrow. Make sure you register early afternoon, before two o'clock."

I got off the phone and ran outside to tell Jerry. Why, I don't know, but it seemed like the best news in three weeks, despite knowing the surgery was rescheduled, not canceled.

As requested, a week later we were registered by two in the afternoon. I considered it a bad omen to be comfortable in the hospital, my comfort feeling like a slow but steady collapse under the tyranny of the medical bureaucracy's brainwashing. But we settled in: inspirational books, tape machine with meditation music, toys for Aaron, our vitamins, and my exercise clothes.

Jerry and I were focused on Aaron, this delightful six-month-old exploring everything he could get his hands on. My only wish was to get him back like this, fully alive, fully experiencing his life.

We looked over to the doorway, a most welcomed sight, the sight of us playing with a product of his creative genius. Dr. Berenstein brought a chair over and sat rather closely.

He leaned forward, his manner intimate. "Would you give me one more try with Aaron? I really think I can close those two arteries now. We've developed a new catheter; it's got the qualities of being both flexible and sturdy. I believe I can get it to stay out of that hairpin turn in the malformation."

I looked into Jerry's eyes and saw what I was feeling in my own heart. I felt blessed. This was a miracle. I was so grateful for this man in whom I had entrusted my son's life. There was a deeply connected feeling between all three of us. No words were required to articulate our intense satisfaction.

"Aaron will still need to have a shunt put in," he said. "With your approval, Dr. Wisoff can do that on Friday, and I can do the embolization the following Monday."

At that point, I didn't mind the idea of the shunt so much. That Aaron was not going to have metal probes doing their duty in the undulating formations of his brain matter thrilled me. I felt like kissing Dr. Berenstein's feet.

"You have our absolute approval," Jerry said.

"Great, I'll go and tell Dr. Wisoff. Good luck tomorrow. It should be a piece of cake." Unlike the last time he left the room, this time he was on his toes.

Chapter Twenty

✳

Aaron was upright in his crib a mere half hour following the completion of his shunt insertion, totally content playing with toys. Quite honestly, I was surprised he was not craving the embrace of his parents' arms as usual, and surmised he was feeling more comfortable in his body, now that the fluid in his brain was properly regulated.

We stayed over the weekend as Aaron's procedure with Dr. Berenstein was scheduled first thing Monday morning. There was cause for much contemplation in the quiet moments of naptime and my daily runs. In our minds, the last-minute replacement of Aaron's neurosurgery with the embolization procedure was an extremely welcome turn of events. That which we feared so desperately was of no concern any longer, synchronicity working its charm in what we considered our favor.

Over the weekend, we discovered that Dr. Berenstein had returned from his conference in France a mere three days after we got bumped from neurosurgery.

Had Dr. Wisoff not had an emergency to contend with, we would not have known about Dr. Berenstein's new and more flexible catheter. Aaron would have had neurosurgery; whether it would have been successful is not even up for speculation.

I thought back on Edie's words from her spirit guide five weeks ago—the part where she commented about simple answers for simple questions and having to look to do things the hard way first. Those words were certainly open for any number of interpretations. I was of the opinion that neurosurgery was the hard way and embolization the easy way. Furthermore, I believed the cancellation of Dr. Wisoff's neurosurgery to be a perfect example of co-incidence, as it created an opening for Aaron to be taken care of by Dr. Berenstein once again. My paradigm for life was being completely validated, my faith in a grander power that be anchored in more deeply than ever. The end was within reach. I just knew it.

Jerry was roaming the halls late one night, looking for children to whom he could bring cheer. He spoke with a Chasidic mother of ten who was in the hospital with her youngest, a five-year-old who was dying of cancer. He noticed a grace about her, a keen acceptance. "God doesn't give you any more than you can handle," she said. "And everything is besherdt, meant to be." She had struggled many years to keep her family close; this youngest sibling's fight for life was a tribute to her, accomplishing what this most gifted mother couldn't. This was the light for her, the thought she focused on through all the suffering she had and would have as time marched on. I was inspired and again thought my struggle to be minute compared to people like her.

Aaron went down to the operating room at nine-thirty Monday morning, Jerry and I, for the fourth time, planting ourselves in the parents' waiting room. The day was fairly non-eventful — no show-stopping revelations this time. I had settled into a fully upholstered arm chair with my book and cup of tea, my back to the door so I wouldn't be distracted by the activity in the corridor. Jerry did just the opposite, lying on a couch facing me and the door, unable to get absorbed in any reading.

The hustle of the morning tests and examinations was over. Lunchtime too. The afternoon came, and the apprehension settled in. This ordeal has aged me, I thought, sinking lower in the chair. I stuck my head back in my book, attempting to bring more constructive thoughts to my mind. The minutes dragged.

It was becoming increasingly difficult to stay focused on my book, and I found myself twisting my neck around to check out the activity in the hallway. I got up and did a few laps around the unit. Back in the parents' room, I sat next to Jerry.

"Did you ask the nurse if she heard anything?" he asked.

"No. I figured if she heard from Dr. Berenstein, she would have come to tell us." Not receiving any news meant that Aaron was alive, but we had no idea how the procedure was progressing.

Jerry looked at me, tears welling in his eyes. "I know, Sweets," I said. "I hope this is the last of it too."

Someone came in to use the pay phone in the room. I stroked Jerry's face and went back to the chair and my book. It was nearing three o'clock, the time dragging on. I immersed myself in my reading, resisting the temptation to look up every time someone passed in the hallway.

Thankfully, my book was absorbing and eventually the noise in the hall dissolved into a background hum. I faintly noticed a slight breeze moving past me from the doorway, but my brain didn't process it as a breeze made by a person walking past me, so I didn't look up.

"It was a success. We got it!" I looked up. It was Dr. Berenstein. Not noticing me, he had walked straight over to Jerry.

I couldn't contain myself. I lunged from my chair and practically pounced on Dr. Berenstein's back, hugging him in the glory of the moment, letting out an excited shriek as I jumped up and down. Shocked, he turned around. "Jeez! I didn't see you there. You scared me to death."

I tried to stand still, slightly embarrassed. "I'm so excited. Thank you so much," I said and gave him a big hug.

"The catheter worked like a charm. We got both vessels just as I planned. Your son will be up from the recovery room in about fifteen minutes, so hang around. I have to go back to do another procedure. I'll stop by before I go home tonight."

Dr. Berenstein left, and Jerry and I sobbed in each other's arms for at least five minutes. Hallelujah! We were home free.

Chapter Twenty-One

✳

Spring ushered a new energy into our lives. Our existence finally back to normal, we happily settled into our routines. It was lunchtime and, as was our routine, Jerry went to pick up Jeff from nursery school while I stayed home in one of my more familiar maternal poses. I so enjoyed my private time with Aaron, cuddled in my rocking chair while he filled himself with my manna.

Rather suddenly, Aaron pulled away, and out of nowhere came his projectile vomiting. He jumped a little bit, obviously stunned. Needless to say, so was I. He certainly hadn't given me any indication that he was sick. He didn't even cry. He behaved as if he was learning about some new thing of which his amazing body was capable. Maybe my milk's bad, I thought. Then I remembered the antibiotics we had had to give Aaron due to a tiny bit of redness I noticed around his shunt ten days ago. I would never have opted for antibiotics for what our pediatrician diagnosed as an ear infection, except for the fact that this one was rather bad and stood the chance of tracking up the shunt and into the brain. It was a dangerous enough situation for me not to opt for my usual holistic approach.

I thought back on Dr. Wisoff's ominous words about shunt malfunctions. Vomiting was the number one sign of which to be aware. Was there a connection?

I grabbed for the portable phone and called our family doctor, my throat constricted with a too-familiar feeling of fear. Thankfully, Jerry returned moments later, only to have the whole family pile into the car to go to Dr. Kenefick's office.

Although Aaron appeared perfectly fine when I strapped him into his car seat, I certainly was not. My mind was racing frenetically, fearful of what this new challenge would entail. Just a few short months ago, I remember thinking our challenges had run their course.

Jerry and I sat in the car with grave faces, not saying a word to each other for at least five minutes. I sensed Jerry's fear. After all, it matched my own.

Nervously, I whispered, "I'm afraid, Jerry. I think Aaron has a shunt infection. I told the nurse about the redness around his shunt. She put me on hold to tell Dr. Kenefick and the next thing I knew, she said to bring Aaron in immediately."

A tear welled in Jerry's eye. "How much more can that little kid take?" he asked, flicking the rear view mirror to look at him.

We were ushered into the pediatrician's office immediately. Dr. Kenefick drew a drop of blood from Aaron's finger, testing it in some high-tech meter right before our eyes. "I think you ought to go directly to NYU. His white cell count is over 27,000. That's indicative of a major bacterial infection."

Obviously, although I had no way of knowing it then, by the time we started Aaron on the antibiotics, the infection had already traveled into his shunt, those microscopic bacteria wreaking all the havoc they could.

One place I never wanted to revisit was NYU Medical Center. "Couldn't we be taken care of at Stamford Hospital?" I asked. I was hanging onto a thread, hoping that this required rather standard hospital procedure. If he said yes, it would be a sign Aaron's condition was not that critical.

"I think you ought to be seen by your own doctors at NYU. I'll call ahead and tell them to expect you."

Crushed again. I hated the thought of going back to NYU. But what could I do? It had gotten to the point where I could go into automatic mode, putting my emotions on hold until I got through the handling of whatever logistics I needed.

In a daze, we rushed home. I contended with dangling pieces of business, handled the care of our home and dogs, and told Jerry what to pack, all with lightning speed. I was frenzied. I imagined the worst. Dr. Wisoff would have to replace Aaron's shunt. More surgery. How long, this time, would we be in the hospital? How long, this time, would I be away from Jeffrey?

Jeffrey loved driving into the city, going over the bridge, looking for airplanes taking off and circling for landing at La Guardia Airport. The children's chatter and playing behind us was a welcome diversion from the bothered thoughts plaguing my mind. Jerry and I were quiet, not voicing our thoughts about this new challenge. What was there to say? Neither of us had any idea of what was in store.

Being admitted through the emergency room of a major metropolitan hospital is as bad as it looks on television, especially when you are not dying. You wait for what seems an endless amount of time. And it is noisy, chaotic, and most surely, intrusive on your psyche.

About four hours after arriving, we were finally admitted. Of course, I had to do some emphatic talking with the clerical people. I couldn't understand why we were just sitting around if this shunt infection was so life-threatening. Eventually, one of the clerks had the good sense to call Dr. Wisoff, a move that finally got Aaron admitted. Out of the zoo to the Peyton Place of Nine East.

Some things just never change. Same nurses, even some of the same patients. By this time, we were very familiar to the nurses. In fact, upon sighting us, they were absolutely stunned. Aaron's previous stays had made him an all-time favorite on Nine East.

Old unit-mates, Beth and her daughter, were like fixtures, endlessly pacing the halls. It was five months since our last hospitalization. Poor woman, the medical staff at this prestigious hospital could not figure out why her three-year-old would not eat.

After all the bloods were drawn, a regimen of broad-based intravenous antibiotics was chosen. This was until the results from the cultures came back, showing what particular strain of bacteria was the culprits.

Jerry took Jeffrey downstairs to be picked up by his folks. Thank God they lived so close and adored Jeffrey so much. I wondered what his three-year-old mind thought about all the time he spent with his grandparents, his mommy spending so much time with his younger brother. This escapade could only enhance the normal struggles of sibling rivalry yet to demand our attention!

While Jerry was downstairs, a nurse came to the room to tell me it was time to put in IV lines to administer antibiotics to Aaron.

No one was in the treatment room when I got there. Aaron, with arms wrapped around my neck, desperately tried to keep his body as close to mine as possible. I cajoled him into sitting on the table as two young-appearing women, the pediatric residents, walked in. Through a thin facade of confidence, I could see their fear, a fear sourced by a general lack of experience, a lack their white lab coats couldn't disguise.

Aaron was lying face up on the treatment table. I was leaning over him, playing with him to keep him calm. This required major effort on my part; after all, these rookies were randomly tying surgical tubing around his extremities, and tapping on his veins. I tried holding steady whatever extremities they weren't working with. This was not a new experience for me. Throughout the hospitalizations, I accompanied Aaron whenever we needed bloods drawn or IV lines established. As usual, it was a wrestling match.

The residents decided on a vein, a juicy one in Aaron's right arm. I lifted my shirt and leaned over Aaron to nurse him. What an act of deceit. I knew what pain they were ready to inflict on his gentle body. I wanted desperately for it to work the first try, afraid they would have to prick him more than this once. God knows, Aaron had enough needles in the eight months he had been on this planet.

Aaron writhed in pain as they probed the needle into his unsuspecting arm. Aaron pulled off my breast, crying. The resident pulled back on the needle, setting up for her next approach into Aaron's mischievous vein. Feeling less pain for a moment, Aaron started sucking again. Jab! Right into his flesh. He screamed in pain, his legs attempting to kick off the hand that held them steady. Again, the resident pulled back on the needle. That vein into which she was attempting to run an IV line slid from underneath the needle four more torturous times.

"I think we ought to try another vein," she said, my mind envisioning her as a butcher... or something worse. This was my son, not a slab of meat! I felt the anger rising inside of me.

When Aaron relaxed a little, they tied the surgical tubing around his right leg. They tapped on his calf, on the inside of his ankle, then on the top of his foot. The residents looked perplexed. It took strenuous effort to keep myself calm in the face of their inadequacy. Where was Jerry when I needed him?

They took the surgical tubing off that leg and put it on the other leg. Then they tapped on this calf, on the inside of this ankle, and again on the top of this foot. They were decidedly not content with the pickings.

Elastic off, and onto the left arm. Aaron was seething in anger at this point. Unhappy with the veins in this arm, the residents went back to the right leg. They strapped the surgical tubing on, tapped some more on the top of Aaron's foot, and decided to go in for the dive. Angry and impatient, I again positioned my breast over Aaron's face. Automatically, he started to nurse; only briefly, however, for once again, he'd been duped. Pulling away from my breast, he let out a scream in complete defiance of this intrusion. My heart was breaking for my child. My stomach was queasy. They continued to probe far too long in my estimation and took the needle out, again unsuccessful.

The residents excused themselves and went out of the room for a minute. Into my arms I pulled up a still-sobbing Aaron, pained and scared, searching for the well-known comfort of my breast. I leaned against the table and let him nurse, calming him, talking to him, and somehow trying to make up for what had just happened. I felt terribly responsible.

The residents came back into the room, their fear speaking even more loudly than earlier. Aaron immediately grabbed onto my neck, this eight-month-old begging not to be put down.

I pried him off of me, laid him down and tried to nurse him on the table. Incredibly aware, he avoided taking my breast from under my shirt, keeping a close untrusting eye on the residents.

I well appreciate how difficult it is to feed an IV

line into a baby. I can accept that it hurts too. With competent doctors, I would have been patient and managed the pain I was feeling for Aaron. But these two residents were anything but competent. If these were the best residents this major hospital could offer, I feared for the future of medicine.

The energy in the room was tense as they negotiated their next approach.

"So, do you think we should try from his right ankle, again?" said one resident to the other.

"I guess we could try," she responded, with constricted optimism.

Were my ears really hearing this? We should try?... I guess we could try? Nothing like knowing what you want, and then moving with confidence to attain your goal. I was infuriated. I knew enough about self-fulfilling prophecies to know I would not allow them to move one step towards Aaron with any needle. Not if my life depended on it.

"Are you serious?" I barked. "We could try?" My tone was all but polite, my rage blatantly obvious. "You seriously think I'm going to let you try putting an IV line into Aaron. Not on your life."

The violation was too much. I swept Aaron off the table and stormed through the heavy metal doors of the treatment room, Aaron clinging to me. This was the first time he had ever been exposed to my rage. I'm sure he was rooting for me. No way were those inexperienced residents going to use my son as a pin cushion to improve their skills.

The poor unsuspecting charge nurse was the

recipient of my quiet explosion. "Those residents had the audacity to even think of trying for another vein without ever so much as a drop of confidence. I want to talk to the head resident. Right now."

That gracious nurse handled me well. She didn't defend my blaming comments. "She's at a meeting right now. I'll get you another resident, one of the more experienced ones." She looked compassionately into my yes. "I promise it won't happen again."

"I will not take anything but the best for my son. Please, get the best person for him." I went back to our room and tried to make up to my whimpering Aaron for the intrusion on his body.

About ten minutes later, the head pediatric resident came into our room. She was at least ten years older than the original residents, much more poised. I immediately sensed her confidence and was relieved.

She asked that I not come into the treatment room this time, explaining she would focus better if I were not in the background cringing. I had to pry Aaron from around my neck as I handed him over to her, full well understanding why.

In the meantime, Jerry had come up from sending Jeffrey off with his parents. He found me pacing outside the treatment room.

"You won't believe what happened while you were gone," I announced indignantly.

"Where's Aaron?" he asked, only to hear his screams resounding through two heavy metal doors.

I dumped all that had happened in the forty-five minutes he was gone, anger and all. He was pained,

pained for Aaron and pained for me having to deal with this myself.

The noise in the treatment room finally quieted and in another ten minutes, Aaron emerged. Taped to the left side of Aaron's neck was the IV line. It looked awful. As Aaron and I reached out to one another, I noticed it was held in place by two tiny black stitches. Apparently they had to cut into the side of his neck to access the vein accurately. Aaron practically jumped from the head resident's arms into my own. Back to home, back to the safety and security for which he yearned. Back to mommy's manna.

Jerry and I inspected this disturbing IV line the head resident ran into Aaron's neck. There was a nice, juicy, and yes, visible vein there, that was for sure. The sight was grotesque but I got to thinking about the good side. All four of Aaron's extremities were free to move, touch, feel, explore, and not get stuck underneath him when he slept. He could really throw his arms around our necks as well.

For the two days it took for the blood cultures to be analyzed, Aaron was placed on a broad-based antibiotic. The culprits isolated, Aaron's medication was changed to a more specific antibiotic, Gantrocyn. Within minutes of its injection, Aaron became incredibly cranky. At the end of the next half hour, he spiked a fever of 101 degrees, throwing himself around in a restless frenzy, refusing all food and toys. I spoke to each white-coated professional who entered our room, and despite my tormented complaints, all I was offered was Tylenol and a seemingly rehearsed reply that Aaron's response was typical. Typical of what? I asked myself. This was my son, not a typical child or situation.

Blood cultures were performed daily, this five-day course of treatment eliciting no change in Aaron's white blood cell count whatsoever. This and my persistent lamentations caused the doctors to opt for another antibiotic, Rosephrin. Fortunately, the fevers backed off, but after three days of this protocol, the white cell count still showed no improvement, results which made no sense.

Against my pleas for humane treatment, the doctors put Aaron on a different fever-spiking antibiotic. We endured for another three days with the help of Tylenol, only to be informed that a more aggressive protocol was needed as the white blood cell count had not been altered. It was day thirteen of this ordeal.

The perplexed team of doctors decided to withdraw shunt fluid, thinking they would find an answer to their quandary. Right through Aaron's scalp and into the shunt tubing, they poked their needle, successfully drawing out a few cc's of clear cerebrospinal fluid. Results from the lab reported no bacteria. Yet Aaron's white blood cell count was still unchanged. Why would there be no bacteria present in the shunt fluid and concurrently be a highly elevated white blood cell count?

So the doctors started a little game to deduce a reason for this conundrum. They stopped all antibiotics for two days. We got our son back, the easy-going, agreeable son we had come to know. They removed some shunt fluid only to find the bacteria again. The enemy had come back.

Yet another fever-spiking antibiotic for a few days and the predictable incessant complaints from Aaron. The doctors tested Aaron's shunt fluid, the bacteria were gone. Yet, his white blood cell count remained where it had.

The white-coats kept invading. More fever-spiking antibiotics and sleepless nights. The clear shunt fluid and elevated white blood cell count continued to haunt the team of doctors attempting to conquer the intruder.

Chapter Twenty-Two

✳

We might as well have taken up residence in our sparsely decorated midtown location. It is nearing three weeks since our admission. Aaron's doctors are entirely perplexed by the behavior of this infection raging war in Aaron's shunt. Me, I'm almost maniacal, desperately grabbing at anything to help my son. I hate the shunt, hate those white-coated doctors who have administered far too ample an array of antibiotics and only causing my precious son tremendous discomfort. With my ingrained holistic tendencies, I keep thinking about how these antibiotics are compromising his immune system and what I will have to do to get Aaron's body in balance after this scientific assault is over. Why can't they pull it together enough to figure out what antibiotic will work?

I'm questioning God's motives, not able to find any good in all that has happened. Why, God? Why are you doing this to my son? What else could you want from this defenseless little being? How bad could his karma possibly be? Hasn't he been through enough already? Haven't I been through enough? What more can I possibly learn? I looked at our situation from every angle imaginable, yet could not discern the purpose of God's actions.

Rounds are typically made first thing in the morning, with surgeons making second visits at the end of the day after their scheduled surgeries or office hours. Dr. Wisoff, who had overseen the entire antibiotic fiasco, unexpectedly graced us with his presence right after lunch one day, a poignant look of purpose on his face. Our reservations about Dr. Wisoff had us on guard.

He said, "Listen, we're not going to be able to overcome this infection unless we remove the shunt from Aaron's head. Every time we administer the antibiotics, the bacteria lodges itself in the shunt tubing, that is, the material the shunt is made of. Then, when the cerebrospinal fluid in the shunt tests clear of the bacteria, we stop the antibiotics. Immediately, those bacteria march straight back and reinfect the fluid. We're going to have to remove the shunt."

Fantasizing my original intention with regards to the shunt, my mind raced, feverishly attempting to compute what he said. Was it possible? How could he remove the shunt when Aaron supposedly needed it to regulate the flow of fluid through his brain?

Dr. Wisoff proceeded to answer my unspoken questions. "After the shunt is removed, we'll put Aaron on a course of IV antibiotics for another ten days. Once his white blood cell count normalizes, we'll insert another shunt."

Mind racing complete, data digested, strategy

formulated. "What if Aaron doesn't need the shunt after the infection is gone," I piped in.

"Mrs. Gershon, once a shunt...." he said.

".... always a shunt," I chimed in.

"Well then, how is Aaron going to manage without the shunt when you remove it?" Jerry said. Jerry and I were on the same wavelength.

Dr. Wisoff's face donned its professor-like veneer. He sighed a deep breath. This was complicated because he needed his hands to help us comprehend what he was about to explain. Present also was an element of uncertainty, what appeared in my mind to be a chance for Aaron to be shunt-free. We sat, riveted to our seats. Vivid pictures flashed in and out, across the screen of my imagination.

"We're going to have a sort of dry run first. What we're going to do is externalize the shunt. By that, I mean we will remove the end of the shunt that's in Aaron's abdomen and attach it to a sterile bag. As long as the bag is lower than the shunt valve in Aaron's head, the shunt will continue to regulate the flow of cerebrospinal fluid." He pointed to the valve, the bulb-like part of the shunt tubing that was adjacent to the point where he drilled into Aaron's skull to place the shunt.

"We'll gradually raise the bag to a level higher than the valve, testing Aaron's vital signs every fifteen minutes to start. If he tolerates the change and his vital signs are steady, we will continue to raise the bag. Once the bag is over Aaron's head and tolerated, hopefully, we can then assume it safe to remove the infected shunt.

We'd do at least one CAT scan during the week and a half he'd be without a shunt and on the IV antibiotics, just to make sure the fluid level in Aaron's brain doesn't increase too much. After he finishes the antibiotics and the blood results come back favorable, we'll insert another shunt."

"What if the fluid in Aaron's brain increases too much while you're raising the bag to the level of the valve?" I inquired.

Somberly he replied, "That would be a big problem. That's why we're doing it in the manner I explained. To keep a close watch."

I heaved a pained sigh, by this time resigned, and wanting only Aaron's comfort.

Within half an hour, the shunt was externalized, and the antibiotics stopped. My son seemed a happy camper. The nurses visited like clockwork, taking Aaron's vital signs, just as Dr. Wisoff said they would. The bag got raised little by little. Aaron was bearing up just fine. Jerry and I waited, tentatively, praying quietly in the private chambers of our minds.

The bag, which was being pinned to the back of Aaron's shirt, over the course of two days, graduated to an IV pole and was hung above the level of the shunt valve. All continued along with no complications. A CAT scan was performed. With the valve inactive, Aaron was maintaining his fluid levels independently.

I yearned to be home. In my mind, there was absolutely no reason to stay in the hospital for another week and a half. Why couldn't Aaron get antibiotics at home, I mused.

Likely this would happen to me. While I day-dreamed, my pediatrician from home telephoned, wanting to find out how we were. I recapped the last three weeks to him along with the plan to have Aaron receive the IV antibiotics.

"Lori, why don't you come home and have one of the home IV nurses give Aaron the antibiotics?" he asked.

"Dr. Wisoff doesn't want us to," I said, "but I'd much rather be at home than here. I think it would be better for all of us, don't you agree?" I yearned for his endorsement.

"I'll call Dr. Wisoff. We have an excellent group of home IV nurses right here in town. You guys will do fine."

Later in the day, Dr. Wisoff came in with double good news: Aaron was to go to the treatment room to have his shunt removed and we were scheduled to go home the next day.

Dr. Berenstein had made a habit of checking in on Aaron periodically. After all, our little chicken was one of his pride and joys. By the time he came in today, it was already late. I was alone, reading a book. Aaron was asleep in the crib. He plotzed himself down on one of the chairs, my tired and overworked visitor.

"So I hear you're to go home tomorrow. I think it's better for you to be at home too."

He's on my side, that's interesting, I thought. Ever since Dr. Berenstein successfully bumped Dr. Wisoff from his once-scheduled brain dissection, Jerry and I sensed a little ego competition between the two doctors. It was a bit comical; however; although they did not always see eye to eye, they appeared to maintain an appropriate interdisciplinary relationship.

Dr. Berenstein and I babbled a bit, back and forth about this most recent hospital experience and his workload. I should have guessed he was hedging at telling me something, some vital piece of information that might be contradictory to Dr. Wisoff's opinion.

He started to rise from his chair. Half-way up from sitting, he stated in a matter of fact manner, "Mark my words, your son will not need a shunt."

By the time he had finished his words; he was turning on his heel and heading towards the door. I lunged forward from my chair, attempting to grab at his lab coat to have him turn around and repeat those lovely words. But I wasn't quick enough.

Adrenaline was racing through my bloodstream at the speed of light, my heart pounding in excitement. "Wait a second," I announced as he approached the door. "Did I hear you right? You can't drop a bomb like that and just walk out."

He turned back, pride radiating bolts of certainty from his eyes. "You heard exactly what I said," and then walked out.

"Wo, yes!" I thundered, throwing my arms in the air as I jumped for joy. I was explosively ecstatic. Could I have done back flips, I would have done ten. All in a row, ending with a grand finale of a one-and-a-half turn spiral twist. Imagine, Dr. Berenstein believed as I... we were going to pull this off. I felt like putting on my best clothes and wildly dancing in the streets, singing a proclamation to the world of God's good grace.

For a brief second, I held my breath. Nothing was definite until the next CAT scan, I thought. But in replaying Dr. Berenstein's words, my fearful hesitation was completely overpowered in a flash, and resurrected was the strength of my inner knowing as it had been the day I rigorously argued with Dr. Wisoff three months ago. Aaron was to defy proven medical statistics and not grow up with a shunt in his head!

As if all the spine-tingling excitement were not enough, something much bigger dawned on me. This expected outcome was a miracle. A bona fide miracle. "Thank you, God," I humbly spoke out loud, and broke down into a most beholden sobbing, once more feeling the unfathomable protective presence around me.

Jerry, who had left to his parents' home to be with Jeffrey only twenty-five minutes ago had just arrived when I called. I relayed Dr. Berenstein's words, he first bellowing his pleasure, and then crying in joy. "Thank you, God," I heard him say to himself. I listened in as he shared our wonderful news with his parents and Jeffrey. What a celebration. What a great life.

Jerry and Jeffrey came to pick me and Aaron up the following day and by lunchtime, we were checked out of the hospital and driving home. It felt like heaven to be a whole family again. Safe from the intruding whitecoats, we were left only with the tasks of anticipating substantiation of Dr. Berenstein's prophecy and praying not to be disappointed.

Chapter Twenty-Three

✳

Instead of the CAT scan, the doctors decided on an MRI which we had done and the results delivered to Dr. Berenstein and Dr. Wisoff, following the course of home IV antibiotics. We held our breaths waiting for the verbal report, praying Dr. Berenstein's words were not solely words of the ego.

Hallelujah! They both confirmed Aaron no longer needed a shunt. Because hydrocephalus was no longer an issue, and the two mischievous arteries were no longer patent, Dr. Wisoff was no longer needed. The orders from Dr. Berenstein: another MRI in six months to follow the fistula, the positive expectation being it would be totally occluded within a few months.

What can I say about all this? I cursed that ear infection with a vengeance and yet it turned out to be the very thing that caused the shunt to be removed. God does work in mysterious ways, I affirmed. How many times in my life had I cursed the circumstances that yielded the most perfect results possible? I thought about my fear, my anger, and my loss of faith.

And look at the miracle.

I reflected on the back and forth conversation with Dr. Wisoff about Aaron not needing the shunt some time in the future. I knew then, Aaron would not need the shunt forever. Somehow, with the shunt infection and the three-week hospital stint, I lost faith, the strength in that knowing. These wonderful circumstances were perceived as obstacles, harshly judged to stand in the way of Aaron's wellness. Another one of life's lessons glared at me, thank God, with the most desired results for Aaron's health. We had come through all this and the battle was over.

Being just a matter of waiting six months until the next MRI to get a clean bill of health, we went back to living our lives with not a care in the world. Aaron's neuromotor development took off. Within five months, he conquered crawling and walking, he and Jeffrey beginning to enjoy their relationship in a way they never could. Jeffrey was a perfect big brother, teaching Aaron everything he needed to know about being a toddler. It was a time of great healing for us.

We were not exempt from life's mundane troubles, but anything we did encounter was kept in perspective and had little or no power over us. When you have been through what we had been through, you look at life through very different glasses, often celebrating the insignificant.

Chapter Twenty-Four

✳

The week before Christmas, 1991. We had gotten another MRI, just as the doctors requested. We hadn't heard anything for two weeks, so I assumed the results were satisfactory. After all, they looked good to me, the fistula about fifty percent the original size and about sixty percent closed. I had become a whiz at reading the MRI film.

Aaron, now seventeen-months-old, was well within the accepted percentiles for growth and development, getting into everything he should not have, like any other child. Jeff, just past four years old, went for a full day of nursery school. Life truly had us back in its flow again.

I had just come home from grocery shopping with the kids. Jerry was out working. As I was putting the food away, the phone rang. The kids, thankfully, were watching Sesame Street.

"Hello, Mrs. Gershon." The high-pitched squealing voice on the other end of the phone was quite intrusive. "This is Mary from Dr. Berenstein's office.

Dr. Berenstein wants you to come in for another procedure," she stated.

I fell back against the wall, stunned. "What? What did you say?"

She repeated herself. I slid slowly, slowly down to the floor, my heart racing. I felt faint.

"But I read the film myself. The fistula is almost closed." I was shaking. "I don't get it."

"You need to calm down, Mrs. Gershon. I am just Dr. Berenstein's nurse. I don't know exactly what he has in mind and I can't speak for him. You get yourself together, a bit. I'll have Dr. Berenstein call you."

She hung up abruptly. Devastated, I stayed on the floor and continued to hold the receiver in my hand, sobbing.

Some time later, I don't remember how long, maybe an hour or so, Dr. Berenstein called. I was panicked, tense. Impatiently, I listened to him, not willing to have it be so. It was a brief conversation. We weren't going to settle anything over the phone. He told me to come in with Jerry and Aaron, next week, Christmas Eve.

Day after day, night after night, Jerry and I talked long and hard about this one. In our opinion, the results on the MRI were favorable. The fistula, although not fully occluded, was well on its way. We couldn't comprehend why Dr. Berenstein wanted to do another procedure. With time, wouldn't it continue to close down? To us it seemed a reasonable expectation.

But what if we were wrong? What if Aaron really did need more work done? What if there were still some patent blood vessels?

Something inside kept tugging at me, tugging at me to let Aaron be. Let go and let God. I processed through everything that had happened with Aaron, how doctors and healers alike helped him. How everything always seemed to be in divine order, the right people at the right time, in the right place. I wanted to trust in Aaron's body's innate ability to heal itself. But what if I was wrong? What if it was my ego tugging at me, rather than a mother's intuitive knowing? This was no small ante we were talking about. If we let Dr. Berenstein work on Aaron again, Aaron could die on the table. More anesthesia and radiation, more blood tests, more aggravation and discomfort. If we chose to not do anything, we risked losing him to a blown-out fistula somewhere down the line. I required an assured victory, no risks at all.

Christmas Eve. Dr. Berenstein's waiting room was filled to the brim with a colorful and noisy array of different ethnicities and nationalities, parents and kids alike. And it was four o'clock in the afternoon, to top it off. Tomorrow was Christmas Day. How in the world would the doctors in this practice see all their patients by the time they needed to get home?

Jerry, Aaron, and I sat down in a corner somewhere, father reading to his son, and mother to have another one of those synchronistic moments of evidence to support her belief in the power that watched over Aaron.

A nicely dressed woman, probably Hispanic, and her sweet four-month-old baby girl sat to my right. "What's wrong with your son?" she asked. For some reason, the code of ethics in a place like NYU Medical

Center allows for such inquiries between complete and total strangers. It's a morose curiosity that needs to be filled. In the end you can be happy your child has what he or she has, not what the other child has.

"He had an arterio-venous malformation at the vein of Galen," I answered.

"Oh my God," she said, "that's what my daughter had. We're here to have her four-month check-up and to schedule another procedure."

"When was her first procedure done?" I queried.

"Two days after she was born. They discovered the AVM in my fifth month of pregnancy on the ultrasound. They had it all planned. The moment she was born, she was taken from me and put on life support."

I sat there, stunned by what I had just heard. How did Aaron survive after he was born? It seemed a miracle his body did not go into distress the moment he was born, as it apparently did with this girl. My God, he was born at home. If he had gone into distress right after he was born, how would he have survived? Again, I experienced that incredible feeling, the absolute knowing of God's watching over us.

"Your daughter looks well. Dr. Berenstein works miracles on these little ones, doesn't he?" I responded.

Jerry rose with Aaron and called my attention. Dr. Berenstein had walked into the waiting room and was looking for us. As usual, he was in a rush. "Come, come. I'm sorry to do this to you. I know you've come a long way. I have an emergency to attend to, so we'll have to talk while you walk with me over to the other building."

We walked out of the reception room and into the hallway. "Listen carefully," he continued. "I know the three of you have been through an awful lot. You're tired of all this. I understand."

"The fistula is almost fully closed and it's almost half the size it was six months ago," I said. "I don't get it. If it's getting better, why do you want to do another procedure?"

"If, in fact, I had closed down all the feeder vessels as I thought I had, the fistula would have been totally closed down by now. But it's not, and therefore, I suspect there are additional tiny feeder vessels that couldn't be seen before I embolized the larger vessels."

"I don't get it," Jerry said, "Why didn't they show up before?"

"Before the larger vessels were embolized, the blood didn't flow through the tiny vessels. The blood moved along a pathway where there was the least resistance to flow. Now that those pathways are shut down, the blood is forced to move through the tiny vessels, albeit at a very slow rate."

We were starting to comprehend what he was explaining. He continued. "Listen, you want to go home? Go home, do your voodoo. Just don't bring him back to me when he's twelve years old. By then he'll have had a major blow-out. I want you to get an MRI done every six months. Wait a year if you guys want, I don't care. Do the procedure when he's three or four years old, even. Just make sure you keep in touch. And get me that MRI in six months. We'll talk then."

And he was off through the double doors to attend

to his emergency. His manner was so rough sometimes and yet he cared so deeply. Maybe it was his passionate Mexican blood. Whatever it was, being the recipient of his paradoxical behavior often left my mind gyrating.

So we went home, just like he said, with plans to do an MRI some time the upcoming summer. We got what we wanted. And hopefully, that next MRI would prove us right.

Chapter Twenty-Five

✳

Some time in the middle of March, I went back to work. We had gone through a lot of our savings during Aaron's first year of life. It was time to start picking up the pieces, as they say.

I felt really torn about working. Ironically, after a five-year hiatus from a not-missed employment with a very conventionally oriented homecare system, there was now, more than ever, a tremendous need for occupational therapists. I went back to my latest of stomping grounds, the Bronx, to do homecare. It was what I knew to do best and it certainly had the best financial potential of all possible rehabilitation settings. Within a month, I had contracts with two major agencies and was receiving cases all over the Bronx, safe and not-so-safe areas. It didn't matter. People who required rehabilitation lived everywhere. We needed money, so I went where they gave me cases.

During the summer, I received a referral to treat a stroke patient. Felix was a Pentecostal minister. Felix, his wife, and his son, were some of the warmest, most loving people I had ever encountered in my work. Enjoying talking spiritual matters with them as much as I did; I often stayed beyond my treatment sessions to ingest the magnificent laying on of hands stories they had to share, for I had come into their home knowing nothing about their religion.

Cindy, my patient's wife, and I got to know one another quite well. Often over tea at the end of my day, she told me many stories of healings and proudly spoke of her son who went into the hospitals to help members of their church.

Two months into his treatment sessions, Felix seemed to be reaching a plateau in terms of his rehabilitation. He was frustrated and angry. More angry at himself, I suspected, and perhaps even at God for having him throw a stroke to begin with. One day, when his anger really escalated, I couldn't help but ask him about his faith, not his religion, but his faith. Cindy walked in on the conversation.

"Why don't you do a laying on of hands for your husband in your church?" She had taken over the ministry during the time he was sick.

"Oh, we have," she said. "Many times. We have healing services in our church all the time."

I felt so close to the family and their problems and had been much more than a therapist to them. Something told me to speak, in that precise moment, for Aaron. "Next time you have a healing ceremony in church, would you please say a prayer for my son?" We are due for an MRI in about a month.

"Of course," Cindy said. After I told her a little

about what had gone on with Aaron, she walked out of the room, in my mind, leaving me with her husband to finish his therapy session.

I transferred Felix back into his wheelchair, and out of the corner of my eye, I saw several people walking into the room. Cindy introduced me to her church friends, who just happened to be having a Bible study session in the other room. She told them about Aaron and they wanted to stop their Bible study short in order to pray for him. I was astonished and agreed to participate on the spot.

An older Hispanic man explained to me in his broken English that he was going to anoint me with oil and use me as a surrogate for Aaron. His brow was already trimmed with beads of perspiration. It was hot in that apartment. It was over ninety degrees outside and no one in the South Bronx has central air conditioning. He put both his hands on my arms, above my elbows. At the top of his lungs, he cried in a pained yearning voice, "Ah Dios mios," (my dear God). All the other people in the room joined in his prayer. "Help this mother's baby," he broke into his battered English. His hands, now clenching my arms, started to tremble. I was wondering why he was shaking me, only to find out later that the Holy Spirit was moving through him and into me. On and on he went, crying out in Spanish for Aaron to be healed. There was such a clamor in the room, each of them speaking words I could not understand. Growing up in New York, I thought I had heard every language imaginable, but this was different. Each person spoke a different language, words which sounded like nothing else I had ever heard. I didn't know what to expect, much less what they were saying. Later, it was explained to me that they were speaking in tongues, a phenomenon common to Pentecostals and their fundamental form of Christianity. It was a different world, unlike anything I had ever seen or heard. Certainly not my contained experience of the synagogue. I laughed at the thought of an experience like this at the conservative synagogue to which my parents took me as a child.

The elder was still shaking me, now sweating profusely, wiping his brow with his sleeve. Although I didn't know what to make of all this, I felt as though I had transcended to a different dimension, my brain entirely fuzzy, my heart overwhelmed with gratitude. The clamor of voices speaking in tongues eventually quieted down to a most profound majestic silence.

The next thing I knew, I was talking into a tape machine about Felix and how he was doing with therapy. His friends asked me to speak in Spanish as best I could because this tape was to be played continually over the radio in their homeland, Ecuador. Tapes would be played for prayer to be given. Pretty amazing, I thought. And quite a lot of people with a lot of focused thought towards the healing of whomever they were praying for. Five years of high school Spanish plus on-the-job Spanish lessons might enable the people hearing the tape to understand what I was saying.

I was urged to tell Aaron's story, my new friends continuing to correct my Spanish as I stumbled around for words to ask for Aaron's healing in as simple technical terms as possible. I was thrilled at the thought of hundreds of thousands of people praying for my son.

I remember walking out of their apartment that day feeling like my feet were five feet off the ground. I kept shaking my head, still amazed at what I had just taken part in. Jerry is not going to believe this one, I thought. More realistically, though, knowing me and knowing what I attract, he would be more apt to say, "I'm not surprised a bit."

I drove home, my head in the cosmos, a grin pasted smack across my face. How was I going to explain this to Jerry? I asked myself. I pulled into the driveway and was greeted as usual by the kids and Jerry. Just one look at the "you won't believe" look on my face and Jerry knew something major had happened. Delirious with joy, I babbled at him, certain my communication was somewhat incoherent.

A captivated Jerry grinned the whole time I told him the story. "Figures," he laughed, "Only my wife would attract something like this." Reminding him we were due for an MRI very soon, the magnitude of what had transpired earlier began to grow on him too. He pulled me into the embrace of his arms, both of us again basking in our growing awareness of God.

Chapter Twenty-Six

✳

I raced from the Bronx up to White Plains, fifteen minutes late to meet Jerry for Aaron's MRI. I had never driven to the medical center from this direction and kept getting lost despite my asking for directions at almost every turn.

I finally arrived, heart racing, to find a wide awake yet dopey Aaron, the chloral hydrate not quite doing its duty. As usual, I took him onto my lap. Aaron, a little more than two years old and still nursing, lifted my shirt and availed himself. In about thirty seconds, his head fell back into the crook of my elbow. The everlasting magic of mother's milk.

I paced back and forth, looking through the technician's window at the computer images. It was hard to follow the rapidly changing pictures while the technicians moved through the progression of images they needed to take. Twenty minutes later, Aaron emerged, sleeping in Jerry's arms.

The radiologist went into his private office to look at the film. I begged him to share his findings with me; after all, quite a lot was hanging on this MRI. The doctor, a rather withholding, insensitive person, wouldn't tell me the results. We'd been getting MRI's there for almost two years. He knew what we were hoping for and how impossible it would be to wait for Dr. Berenstein's report.

"You'll have to wait to talk to your doctor," he said, as he went back into his office. I heard him turn on a tape recorder and begin his dictation. He was barely audible from the chair I occupied along the wall right outside his office. I got up and stood with my back to the wall, right along the molding of his doorway. He was talking about Aaron.

"MRI studies on Aaron Gershon show..." His face peered around the same molding against which I was standing. He stared me right in the eyes, penetrating my assertiveness. Then, quite abruptly, he closed his door.

The technician handed us the film in its usual huge brown envelope. I quickly unlaced the little string that held the folder closed, and pulled out the film. I was barely breathing. Jerry looked on. I went through each of the images. I didn't see a fistula. Jerry didn't either. There was no golf ball-sized circle, partially occluded, as their had been on the last MRI. Our excitement was tentative; after all, we were not licensed to read these exams. Wanting to be absolutely sure and extremely impatient, we asked the office manager to send the film directly to Dr. Berenstein, figuring we'd have a formal report within two days.

Chapter Twenty-Seven

✳

Despite our incessant calls to his office, Dr. Berenstein was not free to get back to us due to an incredibly busy schedule and some travel. Waiting for a bona fide professional to read the results plagued our minds, Jerry and I continually rehashing our interpretations of the MRI and the fistula we didn't see — that is, just to make extra sure we weren't seeing things. Relatively comfortable that all was okay, we did our best to remain calm.

But what if our refusal of Dr. Berenstein's suggested embolization was capricious? What if Aaron really did need more surgical intervention? What if we saw only a partially occluded fistula, while Dr. Berenstein also saw vessels our untrained eyes could not see? What if Dr. Berenstein saw something on this MRI that required treatment? Would we still give nature a chance to finish the healing on its own? How long would we be willing to play with fire in our own way?

These were questions we did not want to address. Not now. Not ever. Nonetheless, they repeatedly arose.

The call finally came, a brief one-minute conversation finalizing two of the most challenging, yet enlightening years of my life. Dr. Berenstein substantiated our findings. "Your son is one hundred percent well. He doesn't need any further procedures. The fistula's totally shut down."

Unconstrained, I yelped a big cheer, not in the least bit considerate of Dr. Berenstein's much-needed eardrums. In my entire life, I had never soared higher. No longer did the pain I had been through matter. In that moment, all of import was the life our healthy two-year-old could now live.

"I wouldn't mind it if you'd send me an occasional MRI," Dr. Berenstein added.

In a second, up went my guard. My mind's flashcard-like images vividly portrayed Aaron's first embolization at a very vulnerable three-and-a-half weeks of age, the devastation of the back-to-back unsuccessful procedures at five months of age, the paralyzing fear of neurosurgery, the shunt installation, the last successful embolization, and the fiasco surrounding the shunt infection. I would not ever want to handle again the heart-breaking stress of any more fevers from intravenous antibiotics, let alone any more hospitalizations. And I was not going to invite anyone to take pictures of Aaron's brain to satisfy the curiosity of any opportunistic or well-meaning doctors — including Dr. Berenstein, to whom I was beyond grateful.

Wrong, I said to myself. Next. No more MRI's for little Aaron. Not one more. We were triumphant. We were free of our ties to the medical establishment.

Politely evading his request, I thanked my dear doctor friend and said good-bye. And good-bye, God willing, to hospitals as well.

Chapter Twenty-Eight

✴

Only in the months following this exhausting experience did the enormous lessons with which I was graced reveal themselves to me. As if building upon a theme, during the many soul-searching hours I spent contemplating this book, what I considered the greatest realization continued to stand out. Not in a conceited way, but in a heartfelt, God-connected way, I dwelled on the notion that my tenacity of thought was perhaps the single most important ingredient in Aaron's achievement of health. It's what I call faith or universal law.

But what about logic? Logic and science tell me that five years ago, being born at home with Aaron's congenital anomaly would have meant death within a few short days. How did he defy logic? Science? Could it be that God, in his infinite wisdom and infinite purpose, chose to use this baby as a test of our faith? For us to know him better? To show us what our faith together with his power could accomplish?

Is it plausible to have met Edie as I did? That she

knew of Aaron's condition? And what about her spirit guides' message for Dr. Berenstein?

When Dr. Berenstein was unsuccessful with the back-to-back surgical procedures and neurosurgery was scheduled, logic tells us we can't have faith, that we've come to our crushing defeat.

Is it pure coincidence we got bumped from neurosurgery and rescheduled one week later, only to find that Dr. Berenstein had been introduced to a new catheter that would three days later prove successful?

Which came first, the ear infection or Aaron's lack of need for the shunt? What would logic say? What might faith say?

Is it mere chance I would have a patient who was a Pentecostal, with dear friends in the adjacent room willing to avail themselves?

Was it concrete reasons that had us decide to deny Dr. Berenstein the opportunity of a fourth surgical procedure on Aaron?

Elusive are the pieces of the cosmic jigsaw puzzle, and especially so when faced with challenges as we were. But there is precision in how it all fits. Faith, desire, intent. They are the primary pieces. Faith is uncanny. That's the wonderful thing about it. All the logic in the world cannot describe faith, nor can it account for the miraculous things that result from it. Faith requires no logic, only our willingness to perceive that which we call God, the strength we carry within us.

From the point in time Aaron telepathically communicated to me, I was resolute in my belief that he would arise a champion. From that specific point in time, my catapultic faith carried me through all the seemingly insurmountable challenges that followed.

Logic would have told me my baby was dead and buried. Faith told me, not so. It comes in the image of a thriving five-year-old triumphant for tying his own shoes.

So where is my faith now?

It's present when we let Aaron swim in the deep end of the pool without parental supervision — I allow my mind to think only that he will be safe.

It's present each time either one of my sons has a fever and we choose, against conventional standards, to treat it homeopathically — contrary to what everyone else believes, I believe that the body has an innate ability to heal itself and I never waver from this belief.

It's present when we discipline in our non-traditional "respectful of the heart" way — even though the behavioral results I seek are not immediate, I firmly know my children are fine individuals. And when the desired behaviors show themselves, they are lasting. So I cling to my knowing during difficult times because I know that to deny the heart is to deny the soul.

It's present in my relationship with Jerry, that even with our seeming impasses, we will feel love again — I have full faith in the power of love to heal everything it touches.

It's present each and every day I live, for I live knowing God will present to us exactly what is needed — I see the evidence daily in the exacting perfection of unplanned incidents making my desires reality.

Faith for me today is my immovable inner conviction that everything is perfect precisely the way it is, and that only what God knows to be the best thing will be provided in due time.

We, God's children, have the capacity to consciously be at cause for the effortless attainment of greatness in our lives. Yes, effortless. Into our God-given freedom of choice, it is imperative we factor detachment, for once our desire and intent, for example, Aaron's wellness, are steadfastly locked into both our own and God's Infinite Mind, we must allow for an abundance opossibilities towards the attainment of these desires to fall into place in their own synchronistic manner, as God decides. In essence, we put it out there, trusting with every cell of our being that our needs will be met, and then we hand it up to God, the Universal Mind, whatever we call the power that infuses our very livingness. It does not matter. And it's supposed to be effortless. In this way only will we arrive as champions with peaceful hearts and fulfilled dreams.

Thank you my child of light for illuminating my life with these pearls.

Child of Light
a true storywritten by
LORI GERSHON
49 Fishing Trail
Stamford, Connecticut 06903
(203) 968-0874

Epliogue

✳

It is 2005. Aaron is fifteen years old, five feet ten inches tall, handsome, strong, articulate, and extraordinarily self-aware. I believe, that due to the circumstances around his birth and infancy and his keen awareness of this part of his early life, that Aaron carries a legacy which is both his burden and his gift.

At around age nine, Aaron presented with blanking-out episodes which were later diagnosed as staring seizures. After consultations with neurologists and many tests, Aaron began taking medicine to prevent these seizures. When Aaron was eleven, an MRI and work-up by Dr. Berenstein, Aaron's original neurosurgeon and neurologist, showed no source of seizures in Aaron's brain. Dr. Berenstein, seeing Aaron for the first time in nine years, was shocked at his size and robust nature. He honestly felt the seizures were nothing to worry about, given all that Aaron had been through. He also commented that since he saw no seizure site on the MRI, it was conceivable that the source of Aaron's seizures was hormonal.

With the exception of the staring seizures and the need for dozens of Band-Aids for falls and scrapes, Aaron has been physically healthy. However, he has not emerged entirely unscathed from his early life-threatening condition. He has been challenged academically because of organizational, fine motor, and visual motor deficits. Functionally, this makes it difficult for Aaron to write either print or script. He has trouble keeping his letters consistently spaced and on the line. Because of his sensitivity to peer pressure and his desire to produce nice-looking finished products, Aaron is understandably very frustrated and oftentimes embarrassed by the appearance of his work. He struggles organizing information for his high school reports, especially when the information on which he reports on is not relevant to his base of knowledge. He feels he is different from other kids, and he is right.

Aaron was persistent in teaching himself to type and boasts "sixty words per minute with only one error," a skill I tell him will serve him well in college. In addition, he has been very fortunate to have some highly talented special-ed teachers. These mentors have had a huge impact on Aaron academically, artistically, socially, and emotionally.

Aaron communicates with a voice that is far beyond his fifteen years. He has uncanny insight into the dynamics of relationships, emotions, and people in general. This gift of insight leaves him hard-pressed to enjoy the innocence and unconsciousness enjoyed by his peers. Like the so-called Indigo Children who have come into this world with a soul contract to enlighten and heal our planet, Aaron's life seems to have that same purpose of worldly magnitude. He has an old-soul quality which presents challenges in his relationships with his peers. I remind him that when he is older, he will be appreciated for who he truly is, especially by the girls. This, of course, makes him blush.

Aaron is certainly my Child of Light. My life is graced by his presence. Through my experience with Aaron, I have learned so much about the role of faith and the power of our minds in designing the very fabric of our lives. Aaron continually blesses my life by inspiring me to expand into the soulfulness of my role as mother and teacher.

Child

of

Light

Purchase this book from your
favorite bookstore, or online from
AuthorHouse, Amazon, Barnes & Noble, Borders

www.lorigershon.com

Printed in the United States
75034LV00001B/1-108